The Resurrection Changes Everything

The Resurrection Changes Everything

Essays in Honor of the Rev. Dr. Herbert C. Mueller Jr.

General Editor
RANDY K. ASBURRY

CONCORDIA PUBLISHING HOUSE • SAINT LOUIS

Copyright © 2024 Concordia Publishing House
3558 S. Jefferson Ave., St. Louis, MO 63118-3968
1-800-325-3040 • cph.org

Manufactured in the United States of America

2 3 4 5 6 7 8 9 10 33 32 31 30 29 28 27 26 25

CONTENTS

INTRODUCTION

For as in Adam all die, so also in Christ shall all be made alive. But each in his own order: Christ the firstfruits, then at His coming those who belong to Christ. (1 Corinthians 15:22–23)

THE resurrection of Jesus Christ is the very lynchpin of all things Christian. It is the axle of the bicycle wheel from which all the spokes of Christian doctrine radiate out to connect with the rim and tire of Christian faith and life. Without the axle, the bicycle wheel simply does not function. Without the bodily resurrection of Jesus of Nazareth, Christianity is either just one of a plethora of meandering man-made religions or it collapses altogether. In fact, if someone truly wanted to undermine the entire Christian faith and relegate the worldwide, two-thousand-year-old Christian Church to the dustbin of history, the task would be quite simple: produce the verified dead body of Jesus of Nazareth.

This simple task, however, has never been performed. Indeed, it cannot be performed. This simple task is impossible because Christ is risen! He is risen indeed! Alleluia! It was this central, crucial confession—that on the third day Jesus Christ rose again from the dead—that inspired Herbert C. Mueller to begin working on a book that would explicate and confess this lynchpin of Christian teaching, faith, and life.

Rev. Dr. Herbert C. Mueller (simply "Herb" to so many) served as first vice-president of The Lutheran Church—Missouri Synod (LCMS) (2010–2019). Before that he had served as president of the Southern Illinois District of the LCMS (1994–2010). Prior to those years of serving the church-at-large he served as parish pastor at Immanuel Lutheran Church, Waterloo, Illinois (1990–1994); Zion Lutheran Church, Bethalto, Illinois (1983–1990); and Mount Calvary Lutheran Church, Chicago, Illinois (1979–1983). In May 2019, Herb received a post-surgery pathology report informing him that he had a glioblastoma multiforme (GBM) grade IV tumor. This necessitated his retirement in August 2019.

In his retirement, Herb began researching and writing a book on the bodily resurrection of Jesus and, by extension, the resurrection of the body promised to all believers in Christ. Herb had long wanted to write such a volume. Drawing from his years of service as pastor and churchman, he sought to "give faithful testimony to the apostolic witness of the bodily resurrection of Jesus Christ from the dead" with the intention "that God will use these reflections for His good purposes." He also desired "to leave something of a legacy of faith and hope in Christ for [his] family, [his] siblings, [his] nieces and nephews and most of all [his] children and grandchildren." (These quotes are taken from Herb's own notes and manuscript drafts.)

His diagnosis with and battle against glioblastoma also led Herb to begin writing his book for himself. Upon reading his pathology report, he said to himself: "Wait a minute, Herb. God has a pathology report too, and He has the last word: 'The wages of sin is death, but the free gift of God is eternal life in Christ Jesus our Lord' (Romans 6:23)."

"Right then and there," he continued, "the question of our title poked its way into my conscience: Herb, do you believe this?"

On March 21, 2020, our resurrected Lord Jesus Christ, in His perfect wisdom, gave Herb a blessed end, graciously taking him from this valley of sorrows to Himself in heaven, delivering Herb from his suffering and giving him rest as he awaits the resurrection of the body on the Last Day. Unfortunately, Herb was unable to bring his book to fruition. Now Herb gives "faithful testimony" to the resurrection by awaiting that resurrection himself.

This book takes up the task that Herb had begun. This volume is neither a biography nor a eulogy of Herb, but it does give thanks to our gracious God for His servant Herb. It is written in loving memory of the life, service, and witness of a dear brother in Christ and a faithful servant of the church. As Herb dreamed of doing in his book, the devotional essays in this book explore and confess the bodily resurrection of Jesus Christ and the resurrection of the body that He promises to all who believe in Him.

The contributors to this book are Herb's fellow servants in the church, including family, friends, and colleagues. Authors are fellow pastors with whom Herb served, both in the parish and in the church-at-large. Some of the pastors are also his relatives—a son, two brothers, and a nephew who is also a godson. Through their "faithful testimony to the apostolic witness of the bodily resurrection of Jesus Christ from the dead," and with selected snippets of Herb's own writing, this volume strives to bring the comforting promise, hope, and joy of Jesus' resurrection to every reader.

Essay titles and themes in this volume are drawn largely from Herb's own "chapter list" of topics that he intended to cover in his book. His chapter list included fifty-three numbered titles plus several unnumbered themes.

Many of Herb's titles, as well as pages that he wrote, clearly envision detailed treatments of Scripture passages that teach the bodily resurrection of Jesus and of His faithful followers. For example, "The Voice of Jesus—Come Out!" would have walked the reader through the raising of Lazarus in John 11. Several titles sought to connect the resurrection of Jesus with other points of Christian doctrine, such as "Resurrection and Baptism," "Resurrection and Justification/Vindication," and "Resurrection and the Lord's Supper." Still other titles indicate that Herb also wanted to wade into apologetics (defense of the faith). Such titles include "Resurrection and Abortion," "Resurrection and Evolution (Engine of Evolution Is Death)," "Skeptics—Answered," and "Limits of Science." A final broad grouping of chapter titles would have centered on pastoral care and practice, that is, how to bring the comfort of Jesus' resurrection into the difficulties, pains, and losses of life in this fallen world. Titles in this grouping include "Resurrection and Human Grief," "Why Did This Happen to Me?" and "The Resurrection and Christian Proclamation."

The contributors to this volume were given the opportunity to select their preferred topic(s) from Herb's chapter list. Where possible, contributors were also invited to consult Herb's own notes and writings. Then our contributors were given the liberty to compose their own versions of the various themes that would have comprised Herb's volume. Essays are written in a non-scholarly, easily accessible style to be edifying for all readers, both clergy and laypeople. Scripture references are included in the text, and many essays include endnotes for further reading, study, and reflection. While we cannot replicate as precisely or as thoroughly what Herb envisioned for his book, we offer these essays as a tribute to the work he began in his brief time of retirement.

Since the essay themes and topics flow from Herb's chapter list, they also nicely organize themselves into the same fourfold groupings that can be discerned in that list. Herb did not explicitly organize his chapter titles in these groupings, but this volume does. Essays in the "Biblical Witness" section focus on various Scripture passages, or groupings of passages, and how they portray and teach the resurrection of both Jesus and His faithful followers. The "True Teaching" section focuses on the connection between the resurrection and other doctrinal topics, such as creation, justification, Baptism, the church, and the intermediate state. The two essays under the heading "Defending the Faith" provide examples of the apologetic task as it relates to the resurrection. The "Joy of Life" essays address the broader application of the resurrection to all of life, especially within the life of the church.

In addition to the original essays by relatives and colleagues of Herb, we also allow Herb to speak for himself. Snippets from Herb's notes and drafts for his book have been selected to highlight or echo what is confessed in the essays. The final essay of this book is Herb's very own swan song, his essay to the 2019 LCMS Convention, which he was most honored to deliver. Even in the early days of his suffering from glioblastoma, Herb gave us all a legacy of faith and hope in Christ under the theme "Joy:fully Lutheran: Rejoice, Pray, Give Thanks."

We begin, then, where Herb's work was stopped. The first feature of this volume is Matthew C. Harrison's "Funeral Sermon for Herbert C. Mueller Jr.," preached on March 25, 2020. While Herb was unable to confess the resurrection of Christ and His faithful people by authoring a book, his years of service, his time of suffering, and now his rest in the tomb all point us to the joys of Christ crucified and risen and His promises of eternal life. Now Herb rests with our risen Lord Jesus, awaiting the resurrection of the body on the Last Day, and we are privileged to take up the task of giving "faithful testimony to the apostolic witness of the bodily resurrection of Jesus Christ from the dead."

Praise the Lord, His reign commences,
Reign of life and liberty—
Paschal Lamb, for our offenses,
Slain and raised to set us free!
Evermore
Bow before
Christ, the Lord of Life adore! (*LSB* 462:4)

Rev. Randy K. Asburry, General Editor
Pastor, Hope Lutheran Church, St. Louis, Missouri
June 29, 2024, The Festival of St. Peter and St. Paul

CONTRIBUTORS

FAMILY IN THE MINISTRY

Rev. Herbert C. Mueller III (son)
Pastor, Immanuel Lutheran Church, Lewiston, Minnesota

Rev. Jacob T. Mueller (nephew, godson)
Pastor, Holy Cross Lutheran Church, Emma, Missouri

Rev. Timothy P. Mueller (brother)
Pastor, St. John Lutheran Church, Nashville, Illinois, and St. Luke Lutheran Church, Okawville, Illinois

Rev. William E. Mueller (brother)
Senior Pastor, Suburban Bethlehem Lutheran Church, Fort Wayne, Indiana

COLLEAGUES IN THE MINISTRY

Rev. Dr. Frederic W. Baue
Pastor Emeritus, St. Louis, Missouri

Rev. Kirk M. Clayton
Pastor, Zion Lutheran Church, Mascoutah, Illinois
Second Vice-President, Southern Illinois District (LCMS)

Rev. Dr. Matthew C. Harrison
Assistant Pastor, Village Lutheran Church, Ladue, Missouri
President, The Lutheran Church—Missouri Synod

Rev. Mark W. Love
Senior Pastor, Trinity Lutheran Church, Toledo, Ohio

Rev. John P. Lukomski
Pastor Emeritus, New Athens, Illinois

Rev. Dr. Scott R. Murray
Senior Pastor, Memorial Lutheran Church, Houston, Texas
Third Vice-President, The Lutheran Church—Missouri Synod

Rev. Timothy J. Scharr
Assistant Pastor, Messiah Lutheran Church, Carlyle, Illinois
President, Southern Illinois District (LCMS)

Rev. Steven C. Theiss
Pastor Emeritus, Frohna, Missouri

Rev. William C. Weedon
Assistant Pastor, St. Paul Lutheran Church, Hamel, Illinois
Host, The Word of the Lord Endures Forever *Podcast*

Rev. Dr. John C. Wohlrabe Jr.
Assistant Pastor, Our Savior Lutheran Church, Whitefish Bay, Wisconsin
Sixth Vice-President, The Lutheran Church—Missouri Synod

ABBREVIATIONS

AC	Augsburg Confession.
ACCS NT	*Ancient Christian Commentary on Scripture.* [New Testament.] Edited by Thomas C. Oden. 29 volumes. Downers Grove, IL: InterVarsity Press, 1998–2007.
AE	*Luther's Works: American Edition.* Volumes 1–30: Edited by Jaroslav Pelikan. St. Louis: Concordia Publishing House, 1955–76. Volumes 31–55: Edited by Helmut Lehmann. Philadelphia/Minneapolis: Muhlenberg/Fortress, 1957–86. Volumes 56–82: Edited by Christopher Boyd Brown and Benjamin T. G. Mayes. St. Louis: Concordia Publishing House, 2009–.
ANF	*The Ante-Nicene Fathers: Translations of the Writings of the Fathers down to A.D. 325.* Edited by Alexander Roberts and James Donaldson. Revised by A. Cleveland Coxe. 10 volumes. Buffalo: Christian Literature Publishing Co., 1885–96. Reprint, Peabody, MA: Hendrickson, 1994.
Ap	Apology of the Augsburg Confession.
FC SD	Solid Declaration of the Formula of Concord.
LC	Large Catechism.
LSB	The Commission on Worship of The Lutheran Church—Missouri Synod. *Lutheran Service Book.* St. Louis: Concordia Publishing House, 2006.
LSCE	*Luther's Small Catechism with Explanation.* St. Louis: Concordia Publishing House, 2017.
SA	Smalcald Articles.
SC	Small Catechism.

THE RESURRECTION CHANGES EVERYTHING

The bodily resurrection of Jesus from the dead is ongoing assurance from God Himself that Jesus Christ is Lord and is worthy of our trust. In a world full of competing voices, our purpose here is to boost your confidence in this heart of our faith, the resurrection of Jesus from the dead. That's because the resurrection changes everything. Anyone who is unsure of the fact that Jesus rose from the dead will also be less confident in other areas of apologetics and witness: creation vs. evolution, the exclusive claims of Christianity, etc. However, when a person is fully convinced Jesus Christ did rise bodily from the dead and that He is alive today, ruling over all creation for the sake of His church, such conviction shows a confidence in the Christian message that is not easily shaken. Certainty about the death and resurrection of Jesus and the reason for it—the boundless love of God—profoundly changes how that person thinks of others and approaches them.

Rev. Dr. Herbert C. Mueller Jr.

FUNERAL SERMON FOR HERBERT C. MUELLER JR.[1]

Matthew C. Harrison

THE text that Herb chose for this day is from Galatians 2:20: "I have been crucified with Christ. It is no longer I who live, but Christ who lives in me. And the life I now live in the flesh I live by faith in the Son of God, who loved me and gave Himself for me."

Dear friends:

Christ is risen. Alleluia.

All of these texts, you know, were chosen by your dad. And there were many others too. He wanted, as you well know, to make a confession of the faith and also to provide consolation for you. That was his wonderful motive.

If I were you, I would get that service, with all of its longer sections. I would put it together and print it as a book: *Herb Mueller's Consolations in the Face of Death*. As we were going through the service, there were so many of those lines from hymns or Scripture that I had heard him quote over the last year from his hospital bed, until the time when his voice became labored and he had difficulty getting them out. That is a great blessing.

Illness, suffering, and death are horrid business. This year has been very emotionally and physically draining for you, Faith, and for the whole family. Death and illness, in all its profound effect upon us, is the evidence of the sin that besets us all.

How profoundly troubling to watch those wonderful, lucid eyes of your husband and dad grow dim when he was losing his sight. His lips that kissed you were growing chapped and rough and white. That wonderful, confident, resonant voice, that many times kept me from going over the edge, became labored and fading and incoherent.

Finally, his hands, his touch. I don't know how many pictures I've seen, Faith, of you walking hand-in-hand with Herb. I don't know how many hundreds of times I've seen it. But that touch has faded and became cold.

But I know Another whose eyes grew dim. The very eyes that wept over Lazarus and looked with pity on the man born blind, the lame, and the sick. Eyes that beheld the troubled and gave people comfort: "In the world you will have tribulation. But take heart; I have overcome the world" (John 16:33).

I know Another who from the cross refused the sour vinegar to wet His lips, the lips that spoke so many blessings: "Come to Me, all you who labor and are heavy laden, and I will give you rest" (Matthew 11:28). Even from the cross these lips prayed for those who crucified Him: "Father, forgive them, for they know not what they do" (Luke 23:34).

I know Another whose voice faltered, and they even misunderstood what He was saying: "He is calling Elijah" (Mark 15:35). No, He wasn't. He was reciting the first verse of Psalm 22: "My God, My God, why have You forsaken Me?" And He knew exactly why He was speaking that prophecy of the crucifixion that ends with the great Gospel promise: "They shall come and proclaim His righteousness to a people yet unborn, that He has done it" (Psalm 22:31). He had strength for only one verse.

That marvelous voice with divine confidence that shouted "Lazarus, come out!" (John 11:43) and the dead man emerged, that voice finally managed to say only one word in Greek: "It is finished" (John 19:30).

And those wonderful hands of Jesus that blessed the little children—"Then children were brought to Him that He might lay His hands on them and pray" (Matthew 19:13)—those hands were now bloodied and torn and nailed.

I've struggled over all this, and I'm sure you have too. Your dad had given most of his life in service to Christ and His church. I didn't want him to retire. But he knew it was time to pay attention to you. He loved you all dearly, very dearly, Nathan, Carrie, and Bert, as well as your spouses and families. I think the only times I saw him weep were the times when he was telling about some pain or challenge you were going through. He loved you dearly, and you know that. It's kind of ironic; he spent so much time in service that you felt his distance from all of you from time to time. He was a workaholic. That's how God built him, I think. Isn't it interesting how God worked him so He would give you Herb this last year? I'm thankful for that.

He was a sinner. He knew it, and he'd confess it every day. He knew all of Luther's lines: "I'm a maggot sack." "I'm a poor, miserable this-or-that." And he believed it.

God doesn't act according to our reason. It seemed to me, of anybody who could possibly be said to deserve a long retirement with his wife and family, it was this man. But God doesn't operate according to our mathematics and our logic. And we know that. God is acting according to His cruciform calculations. And Galatians 2:20 lays it out. "I have been crucified with Christ. It is no longer I who live, but Christ who lives in me. And the life I now live in the flesh I live by faith in the Son of God, who loved me and gave Himself for me."

The New Testament teaches something wondrous. When Paul says, "I have been crucified with Christ," he's talking about Baptism: "We were buried therefore with Him by baptism into death" (Romans 6:4), as we just recited at the beginning of this service. Baptism makes us contemporaneous with Christ. I am baptized with Christ. It clothes us with Christ. Baptism puts us together with Jesus. It puts us in His blessed cruciform arms, with His arms around us. And when the Father sees me, He barely sees me at all. He sees Jesus! And Jesus says, "This is My Herb. He's perfect. His sins are forgiven in Me. He is Mine forever." And it's the same thing with you. You are baptized into Christ. The Father sees only Jesus, His perfect one, His perfect Son, fulfilling all the Law, perfectly balancing family and work, making all the perfect decisions, loving, as He should, all the time, forgiving all, covering sins, covering failings, covering evil thoughts, covering challenges and fissures in families. We're all sinners; we all have them.

Jesus says to the Father: "This one has been crucified with Me. This Herb, he no longer lives. But I, Christ, live for him and in him and before You. And the life Herb now lives he lives in Me. I love him. I gave Myself for him. He is Mine. End of story." Or not quite . . . .

The crucifixion of Christ was on divine purpose. "The blood of Jesus [God's] Son cleanses us from all sin" (1 John 1:7).

This death of our beloved Herb was on divine purpose. Our lives are "hidden with Christ in God" (Colossians 3:3). We might not know exactly what God is doing; we often don't. But we know the promises: "All things work together for good" (Romans 8:28); "Neither death nor life . . . will be able to separate us from the love of God in Christ Jesus" (Romans 8:38–39).

Although I want to ask God in heaven a few questions about this one, I do know this. This death does what death does for Christians. It gets our attention and places upon our minds things we would not otherwise think about, things that actually matter most, such as being forgiven and reconciled, being a family, loving and treasuring one another as precious gifts, being patient with one another's faults, growing in faith, growing in hope, growing in love, right smack in the middle of terrible crosses.

Going to church may be very hard for you for a time. You are going to struggle with emotions, and they're going to come at you at the most unexpected times. There's going to be pain. You will feel joy at times, thankfulness, sorrow. There will be moments when you pull out your phone, thinking, "I've got to talk to dad about this; I've got to share it with him." And all of a sudden, you'll realize you can't do that. There may be depression as reality takes hold. In this struggle, Christ is yours. He's told you, "I've got a hold of you." "If in Christ we have hope in this life only, we are of all people most to be pitied" (1 Corinthians 15:19). The life you live is the one you live by Baptism and faith in the Son of God.

Paul says, "If we have died with Christ, we believe that we will also live with Him" (Romans 6:8). Christ rose from the grave. As Luther says, so much has been done. Christ is the firstfruits to rise again; He's the first one to rise from the grave. That's the hard part. The hard part in a birth is the head. Christ is the Head of the church. After the head is born, the baby comes quickly and easily. That's the way Luther spoke about the resurrection. He said that the work is all done. In fact, it's so far done, we have only one toe still hanging over the grave. Not even a big toe; it's a little toe hanging over the grave. And at the last, the trumpet will blow and Christ Himself will raise us all from the grave.

Christ is risen, and you shall see Him on your Easter, our great Easter.

You shall see those eyes, the eyes of the Son of God, who said, "I am not a ghost!" (see Luke 24:39). You shall see those lips: "Peace to you!" (Luke 24:36). You shall hear His voice: "For a spirit does not have flesh and bones" (Luke 24:39). You shall see His hands: "Come, touch them. See the place where the nails were!" (see John 20:27). And this very body, these bodies, shall rise in Christ!

And what's more, you shall see your father's eyes again. You shall be kissed by his lips again. This is the radical teaching of the New Testament and its teaching of the resurrection. You shall hear that great, wonderful voice once more, shouting with delight: "You're here! I've been praying for you!" We're told in the Bible that we shouldn't pray to saints, but our Augsburg Confession says we should have no doubt that the saints in heaven are praying for us (Ap XXI). Count on it. Your dad and your husband are praying for you. And you, Faith, will grab his hand in joy with Christ, for eternity.

"If it were not so," Jesus says, "would I have told you?" (John 14:2). And for now, "the life I now live in the flesh I live by faith in the Son of God, who loved me and gave Himself for me" (Galatians 2:20).

Christ is risen! Alleluia!

Endnotes

1 Editor's note: The Rev. Dr. Herbert C. Mueller Jr. was called to his eternal rest on March 21, 2020, and the service of Christian burial for him was held on March 25, 2020. Because of the COVID-19 pandemic and government-mandated mitigation measures, the funeral was private and small. An abbreviated version of this funeral sermon appears in Matthew C. Harrison, *Take Courage: Encouraging Words for Discouraging Times* (St. Louis: Concordia Publishing House, 2023), 133–36. This fuller transcript of Pastor Harrison's sermon uniquely proclaims the resurrection by connecting selected physical details of Herb Mueller's suffering and dying with the suffering and death of our Lord Jesus Christ. Since Christ has risen bodily from the dead, He will also give new bodily life to Herb and all who live by faith in Him.

BIBLICAL WITNESS
REMEMBER JESUS CHRIST

A brief personal word about this book: attempting a book could be a sign of pride or rank foolishness. However, this book springs from a lifetime of pastoral experience and reflection.

It is a book I have thought about writing for a long time. Now, in retirement, God has given me more time to work on it. As I write, however, I am praying that the Lord would protect me from the hubris and idolatry of thinking that I will have the argument to convince the skeptic, to console the grieving, or to strengthen the doubting. My prayer is simply that by writing I may give faithful testimony to the apostolic witness of the bodily resurrection of Jesus Christ from the dead. Honesty requires that I also admit to a desire to leave a legacy of faith and hope in Christ for my family, my children, and my grandchildren. This is what it is all about! Jesus lives! By His death and resurrection, He has won the victory even over our final enemy, death itself.

To be sure, it was a sobering thing in May 2019 to read my own pathology report. "Glioblastoma multiforme grade IV" were the words that stood out. Upon reading this, I said, "Wait a minute, Herb. God has a pathology report too, and He has the last word: 'The wages of sin is death, but the free gift of God is eternal life in Christ Jesus our Lord' " (Romans 6:23). The central question is "Do you believe this?" That question will intrude on our story time and again. The question comes from the account of the raising of Lazarus from the dead in the Gospel of John (John 11:26).

Not to mess too much with the work of the Holy Spirit, my prayer is that, together with Martha, we respond, "Yes, Lord; I believe that You are the Christ, the Son of God, who is coming into the world" (John 11:27).

How shall we proceed? The greatest of Jesus' signs in the Gospel of John, the raising of Lazarus, is the sign which was like a huge arrow pointing ahead to Jesus' own resurrection. . . . This will lead also to further pastoral and theological reflection around the central theme of this book, namely, that Christian faith really makes no sense at all without a true bodily resurrection of Jesus from the dead.

Rev. Dr. Herbert C. Mueller Jr.

THE CASE FOR THE RESURRECTION (JOHN 11–21)

Herbert C. Mueller III

THE bodily resurrection of Jesus is central to the understanding of the Gospel of John. The comfort that Jesus offers twenty-first-century Christians is rooted in His first-century words and actions. The Comforter brings the peace that Jesus spoke and did in all these words and actions for us. What He accomplishes in His resurrection thus directly impacts our lives in the present.

Take some time to read through John 11–21. These chapters are filled to the brim with comfort. For the sake of this essay, we will focus primarily on chapters 11, 16, and 20. First, we will examine Jesus' claim for Himself, which is also a claim on us all. We will take this claim and see how it impacts the Christian life directly, especially as the Christian endures persecution and marginalization. We will take this claim to our prayers and fight against the unbelief that says our prayers are not heard. The claim of Jesus expands our experience of suffering and death to the ultimate dimensions of the one who conquers suffering and death with His own suffering and death.

"I Am the Resurrection and the Life." John 11:25

In John 11, Jesus makes the startling claim: "I am the resurrection and the life. Whoever believes in Me, though he die, yet shall he live, and everyone who lives and believes in Me shall never die" (John 11:25–26). Then He backs up that claim by raising Lazarus from the dead: "He cried out with a loud voice, 'Lazarus, come out.' The man who had died came out, his hands and feet bound with linen strips, and his face wrapped with a cloth. Jesus said to them, 'Unbind him, and let him go'" (John 11:43–44). Jesus' claim is both a claim about Himself and a claim of faith on you. As He claims to be the resurrection and the life, He claims the right to raise whomever He wants. When He says "whoever believes," He claims all those who trust in His salvation.

This twofold claim and the resurrection of Lazarus were together the tipping point for those who opposed Jesus. Before this, they had plotted against Him. But after this, they knew that they needed to put their plans into action. Jesus did this miracle the week before Holy Week. The raising of Lazarus had been done so publicly that many people witnessed it. Many people heard about the miracle, and they came to see Lazarus. The man who was dead but was now alive again was such an effective witness that "the chief priests made plans to put Lazarus to death as well, because on account of him many of the Jews were going away and believing in Jesus" (John 12:10–11).

Jesus' claim "I am the resurrection and the life" is central to the Gospel of John, central to the Christian proclamation, and central to the Christian life. Jesus is quite literally the only hope for the world. As the church endures marginalization and persecution, the resurrection of Jesus is a constant reminder that our hope is not of this world, that Jesus has triumphed over all, and that there is a new era in our relationship with God.

"They Will Put You out of the Synagogues." John 15:26–16:4

We begin with the heavy topic of persecution and marginalization. The bodily resurrection of Jesus Christ from the dead is at the heart of the church's witness and her hope in the midst of persecution and marginalization. On the night our Lord Jesus was betrayed, He told His disciples: "I have said all these things to you to keep you from falling away. They will put you out of the synagogues. Indeed, the hour is coming when whoever kills you will think he is offering service to God. And they will do these things because they have not known the Father, nor Me" (John 16:1–3).

We can all agree that it was necessary for Jesus to speak this way to His disciples. They were about to have their faith in Jesus tested. They were about to see their Lord sweat droplets of blood as He prayed in the Garden of Gethsemane. They were about to see Him arrested, put on trial, convicted, scourged, crucified, killed, and buried. Given what they were about to witness, Jesus' words take on even more meaning: "I have said all these things to you to keep you from falling away." Yes, the disciples needed Jesus' words to keep them from falling away. They needed to hear that He was going to send another Comforter, the Holy Spirit, to help them. They needed to know that what Jesus was about to go through was for their good. All this was said so that when the hour of Jesus' enemies finally comes, His disciples would be able to hold fast to His words.

We, however, live on the other side of Easter. We know the end of the story. We know that on Easter Sunday, Jesus rose from the dead, triumphant over sin, death, and the power of the devil. We know that this victory is not only for the disciples back then, and not only for Jesus, but it is for us to share in as well. Still, there is much difference between the victory we know by faith and the way the world is today. We need these words too so that we gain strength of faith from them.

The world of Jesus' day is not so different from today. Jesus is right to tell us as well: "I have said all these things to you to keep you from falling away." He is right to tell us that being a Christian in this world is not always an easy road. There are various attacks on our faith and our witness. I will mention two.

First, there is the attack of apathy. About two decades ago, journalist Jonathan Rauch wrote about something he called "apatheism." By this he meant a theism, a belief in God, that was apathetic, that didn't care about the belief or nonbelief of others. He thought this was a great thing. He found that even those who are intensely religious can be "apatheistic," describing friends who attended church and talked about faith but had no reaction to his overt atheism and homosexuality.[1] They didn't care, they were apathetic, about witnessing to Jesus' death and resurrection. They were apathetic, they didn't care, about calling this man to repentance and faith in Jesus. Why is this?

We could blame the world for this, saying that these Christians know what would happen to them if they spoke up. The world would mock them. They would put their friendships in jeopardy. Their relationships with their unbelieving family members would be at risk. So they say nothing. But is the fault with the world? Or is the fault with the lack of Christian conviction? Jesus says, "But when the Helper comes, whom I will send to you from the Father, . . . He will bear witness about Me. And you also will bear witness" (John 15:26–27). Can Christians remain Christians without bearing witness? That is a good question. We should all search our hearts and repent of our own "apatheism" in witness.

The second and related issue is religious pluralism. This is the idea that it does not matter what God you worship, as long as you are sincere. You hear folks say, "There are many roads to God" and "You have your Christian truth; I have my own truth. It works for me; your truth works for you." However, the claims that Jesus makes in the Gospel of John are exclusive. And they are not made based on whether or not they work! He says, "I am the way, and the truth, and the life. No one comes to the Father except through Me" (John 14:6). The world today would label anyone who made such an exclusive statement as intolerant. Is it intolerant to tell a man drowning in the ocean: "Hold on to the life preserver. It's the only way you'll be safe until we turn the boat around and rescue you"? Is it wrong for the firefighter to tell the person trapped in the fire: "Follow me. I know the only safe way out of the building"? Is it wrong for the doctor to tell his patient: "You are sick, but taking this medicine is the only way that you will recover"? We accept these situations readily enough. Why would we doubt Jesus, who is saving us from the ocean of our sins, from the fires of hell, and from the darkness of eternal death?

Jesus tells us that there is no safety or security for us outside of His Word. You have been given a great gift: you have God's Word. God the Holy Spirit has brought you to faith in Jesus, the Savior of the world. You know the Father and His Son, Jesus Christ, by faith.

The world in Jesus' day thought this Word was peculiar. They threw the disciples out of synagogues, and those such as Saul of Tarsus, who killed His disciples, thought they were offering service to God (see John 16:2). Saul held the coats of those who stoned Stephen to death (see Acts 7:58). It is a frightening thing to be branded a heretic. It is a frightening thing to have the disapproval of the world against you. Mark it well: if we are sincere about our faith, if our only security is in the Word of God, then this is how the world will think about us and how it will react to us.

But Jesus gives us His Word. He has told us that we are truly blessed when others say all sorts of hateful things about us on account of Him. He tells us that when others do this, we are not to respond in kind. We are to pray for those who persecute us. He tells us that we are to love those who hate us. Our love is but a reflection of the love of God: "In this is love, not that we have loved God but that He loved us and sent His Son to be the [atoning sacrifice] for our sins" (1 John 4:10).

Surely the world hated Jesus before it hated His disciples and His Christians. But we need not fear! Our dear Savior Jesus no longer sweats droplets like blood in Gethsemane. He is no longer under arrest. He is no longer on the cross. He is no longer in the tomb. He is risen from the dead! He has ascended to the highest rule and authority in heaven, on earth, and under the earth. He is in charge, and He rules for the good of His Bride, His dearly bought people of God. His Word goes out, calling all people to repent of their sins and to trust that He has worked forgiveness, eternal life, and salvation for all. Saul of Tarsus no longer persecutes the Christians. His whole life was changed by the Lord Jesus when Jesus met him on the road outside of Damascus and said, "Saul, Saul, why are you persecuting Me?" (Acts 9:4).

Notice that the Lord Jesus counts all persecution of His Christians as persecution of Himself. He knows our struggles as we often are feeble and fainthearted in our witness. So He provides strength. His Word is sure, even if we fail to speak it. His witness continues, even if we are silent. In fact, if we do not speak, the very stones would cry out (see Luke 19:40). He knows our sadness when we encounter resistance to the Gospel among our friends, family, and neighbors. He knows how to give us friends, family, neighbors, even more, both here on earth and in the life to come, to compensate us for our loss (Luke 18:29–30). He knows exactly what we need to suffer so that we are kept in the faith as long as we are here on earth. And He will bring us through. "Christ is the world's Redeemer, the lover of the pure" (*LSB* 539:1).

The Lord Jesus has purified you through His blood. He has forgiven you all your sins. He has opened heaven's doors for all who would believe. This truth of the bodily resurrection of Jesus renews our life of witness and love to our neighbor, even if we are thought peculiar, even if they throw us out of the synagogues and think they are offering service to God by persecuting us.

"Whatever You Ask in My Name" John 16:23–33

Christians can be confident that God will answer their prayers because of the bodily resurrection of Jesus. Picture for a moment the child crying for food in the middle of the night. She needs her mother. What will her mother do? God knows: "Can a woman forget her nursing child, that she should have no compassion on the son of her womb? Even these may forget, yet I will not forget you. Behold, I have engraved you on the palms of My hands" (Isaiah 49:15–16).

It is a comfort to know that God the Father hears our prayer based on what Jesus has done for us. I remember that when I was a child my mother would feed us with exactly what we needed. We did not have to ask with long petitions for her to give us something to eat. We did not have to make all our friends ask her to feed us. In fact, she would often make us sit down at the table and eat together. Oftentimes prayer is presented as something we need to do to "bend God's ear to us." We make sure we have enough people praying for us, and God surely must take notice. Or sometimes we present prayer as if we need to "warm God up for us." We use many words to make God happy with us. But the simple truth is that one person praying a short prayer in faith is effective, while hundreds of thousands of folks praying out of their unbelief are not going to be heard. Jesus tells us that we simply ask as beloved children ask their dear father, knowing that God the Father will grant us what He knows that we need.

What has Jesus done for us so that God the Father hears our prayer? Jesus Christ has overcome the world. Jesus Christ has overcome our sinful flesh. Jesus Christ has triumphed over all of Satan's power. That's why He came into the world in the first place. Jesus says, "I came from the Father and have come into the world, and now I am leaving the world and going to the Father" (John 16:28). This event, Jesus' coming from the Father and going to the Father, has given those who believe in Jesus confidence to pray.

What is Jesus' teaching when He says, "I came from the Father and have come into the world"? He is saying what we confess in the Second Article of the Apostles' Creed. We believe in "Jesus Christ, true God, begotten of the Father from eternity, and also true man, born of the Virgin Mary."[2] To save us from our sins, the Son of God took on human flesh in the womb of His mother. There He began His saving work. He brought all of God's commands into human flesh. This is a marvelous mystery revealed to us in Holy Scripture—God the Son, the Second Person of the Holy Trinity, became man and yet remained God. "The Word became flesh and dwelt among us" (John 1:14). He left His throne on high to come and live with us. He came and pronounced forgiveness for sinners, grace for the repentant, and peace with God in His kingdom. All these things were based on what He would do for us on the cross.

Jesus says, "And now I am leaving the world and going to the Father." How does Jesus leave the world and go to the Father? It is through the cross. There, at the cross, Jesus took all our sins, all our punishment that we deserved from the Father, all our guilt, and He suffered it all there. Jesus Himself says this: "And as Moses lifted up the serpent in the wilderness, so must the Son of Man be lifted up, that whoever believes in Him may have eternal life. For God so loved the world, that He gave His only Son, that whoever believes in Him should not perish but have eternal life" (John 3:14–16). Jesus was lifted high, suspended between heaven and earth for you. Jesus has become the bridge between heaven and earth, and through Him, through His death for all our sins, we have access to the Father in heaven. We can, as Jesus says, ask the Father, and the Father will give us what we need, especially forgiveness, life, and salvation. Our prayer is based on Jesus' suffering, death, and resurrection.

Because Jesus Christ has done and is doing all of this, He can say to His disciples and to you: "Take heart, be of good cheer, rejoice, for I have overcome, I have won the victory, over the world, the sinful flesh, and all of Satan's power" (see John 16:33). You can be absolutely sure of this fact. Christ's death and resurrection confirm it. He has ascended into heaven to rule all things for the good of His church.

Our God actually exists. He came to this world. He suffered for our transgressions. He rose from the dead. He is coming again to judge the living and the dead and to give those who love Him life everlasting. His cross and His resurrection show us that He has surely loved us and even the whole world.

"To My Father and Your Father, to My God and Your God." John 20:1–18

When our resurrected Lord Jesus met Mary Magdalene that first Easter, the words He spoke to her show us that we have entered a new era in God's relationship with us. In short, Christ's resurrection has changed everything. Jesus told Mary to go and tell His disciples: "I am ascending to My Father and your Father, to My God and your God" (John 20:17).

Before Jesus died and rose from the dead, we were estranged from our God and Father. The fault was not on His end; it was all on ours. We rebelled against Him. Sin brought us separation from Him who is life. This separation would always come to its supernatural end in death and damnation. Your sinful flesh, which you inherited from Adam, your first father, brought this upon you. What is more, you confirmed that sinful flesh and separation with many more sins of thought, word, and deed.

But now, one of our own, a Brother with flesh like ours, has triumphed! He suffered for our sins on the old rugged cross. Doing that meant taking all that would separate us from the Father upon Himself. He took our lying, our cheating, our stealing, our anger, our hatred, our murder, our adultery, our shame, our disgrace, our hard-heartedness, our unbelief, our hatred upon Himself there on the cross. He cried out under all of that: "My God, My God, why have You forsaken Me?" (Matthew 27:46). Whatever it took, that's what

He did to bring us back to God. He was the only one who was able to do this for us, being true God and also true man.

Now, after three short days, Christ is risen! We say that in the present tense because His bodily resurrection continues. He is risen to ascend to the Father's side, so that one of our own, our big Brother, might plead for us to the Father forever. He sits at the right hand of God's power and majesty to assure us forever of our salvation. He bears that same human nature, a nature like ours, to the Father's side so that we might know that we, too, can call God "Father." We are redeemed by the blood of His Son, our Savior and Brother. He bears the nail-pierced hands and feet and the spear-pierced side to the Father's side so that we can be sure that all our sins and wickedness will never rise again to condemn us. He brings the flesh and blood that was dead but now lives forevermore all the way to the Father's side so that we can be sure that death, even our death, is undone through His resurrection. He brings His victory over sin, death, and the power of the devil all the way to heaven's gates so that we can rest assured in His victory.

In all the trials and struggles of this life, we have a powerful ally in Jesus, our resurrected Lord. He gives us the right to pray: "Our Father, who art in heaven, hallowed be Thy name, . . ." He brings His resurrected body to His Father and our Father to secure the right to pray in this way. We are invited to pray for anything, even our heart's desire, all the while saying, "Thy will be done," and knowing that our Father will give us what is good. We pray because Christ is risen!

When our sins assail us, when Satan attacks us in temptation with the dying gasps of His gloomy empire of darkness, we have a powerful ally in Jesus, our resurrected Lord. When we are tempted, He is able to help us because He Himself was "tempted as we are, yet without sin" (Hebrews 4:15). He knows our weakness and therefore is able to strengthen us for the fight against sin. He continually forgives and covers us with His righteousness. We forgive and are forgiven because Christ is risen!

When death itself comes knocking, either for us or for one of our loved ones, we have a powerful ally in Jesus, our resurrected Lord. We can lay our loved ones to rest in their graves in the sure and certain hope that just as Jesus is risen from the dead, so too will they who believe in Jesus rise to life incorruptible. We can face our own death as Jesus quells our fears with the good news that He is our risen Savior. Death itself may have a toehold on us, but it will not be able to hold on to us for long. We can live with one foot out of the grave already, knowing that no matter what happens, Jesus, our Savior, gives life and peace with God to us with His nail-scarred hands. We will rise because Christ is risen!

The grave had indeed been robbed that day. But it was not the disciples nor the chief priests nor the Pharisees who took Jesus' body away. Christ robbed the grave of all its power. Christ robbed the crown from the devil's pale brow. Christ robbed life away from death. Christ defeated the devil and gave us the true gift of life forevermore. Christ is risen! He is risen indeed. Alleluia!

"Receive the Holy Spirit." John 20:19–31

The world needs the words that the Holy Spirit gave to St. John the evangelist concerning the bodily resurrection of Jesus Christ. Why? First, a little history. Before 1914, the zeitgeist—the social mood of most folks in the world—tended toward the progressive. New products, new modes of transportation, new ideas were making the world a very different place. Everyone was optimistic. The church picked up on this optimism as well, stating that the entire world would be won for Christianity in the next century. The mood was one of triumph, exaltation, man's dominance over the whole world. We were full of pride in our accomplishments.

However, all this unbridled optimism met with a brutal crushing end with the killing fields of the First World War. The zeitgeist was dashed to pieces. The churches throughout Europe were marshaled in support of the states who were at war. Christian killed Christian across no-man's-land. It was a catastrophe in spiritual, economic, social, political, and military terms.

Out of this, though, came a few small voices of Christians who realized that it was human pride and ego that brought this calamity on the world. One such voice was a man by the name of Edward Shillito, an English minister. He wrote this amazing poem that talks about our need for a bodily resurrected Savior. The poem is called "Jesus of the Scars":

> If we never sought, we seek Thee now;
> Thine eyes burn through the dark, our only stars;
> We must have sight of thorn-pricks on Thy brow,
> We must have Thee, O Jesus of the Scars.
> The heavens frighten us; they are too calm;
> In all the universe we have no place.
> Our wounds are hurting us; where is the balm?
> Lord Jesus, by Thy Scars, we claim Thy grace.
> If, when the doors are shut, Thou drawest near,
> Only reveal those hands, that side of Thine;

We know today what wounds are, have no fear,
Show us Thy Scars, we know the countersign.
The other gods were strong; but Thou wast weak;
They rode, but Thou didst stumble to a throne;
But to our wounds only God's wounds can speak,
And not a god has wounds, but Thou alone.[3]

In the last verse of his poem, Reverend Shillito diagnoses the problem we all face. The "other gods" are man-made idols that we view as strong. In his day, they were militarism, progressivism, and nationalism. People had placed their trust in them, but they disappointed. The only God with wounds is Jesus, the Savior.

Today's man-made gods are no different: science, medicine, government, entertainment. They, too, will disappoint us. Still, the God with wounds comes to His disciples. He comes to our world. He comes to you. He comes to show His wounds, to proclaim His peace, and to bring His forgiveness to you.

That first night after the resurrection must have been filled with a strange mixture of surprise, doubt, and fear. The women gave their report: the tomb was empty! Mary Magdalene had told the disciples what Jesus had said, "Go to My brothers and say to them, 'I am ascending to My Father and your Father, to My God and your God'" (John 20:17). But still they doubted; still they were afraid. Their doubts corresponded with their fears. They locked the doors because they were afraid of the Jews, the chief priests, and the Pharisees.

Our world can also resonate with the disciples on this occasion. Now, more than ever, we are fearful. Our fears reveal the gods that we serve, the strong gods that Reverend Shillito talks about in his poem. We fear when our gods are under attack: health, family, money, government, life. These are all good things when received as gifts from God. But when we look to them for salvation, for ultimate safety and security, we go too far. We serve other gods. We fear, love, and trust in other things of our own making. Our doubts correspond to our fears. God said He would protect me from every evil of body and soul, possessions and reputation. Where is that now? God said that He would never leave me nor forsake me. How about now?

To His fearful disciples Jesus came. Even though the doors were locked, He stood among them in the flesh. The first words out of His mouth bestowed peace: "Peace be with you" (John 20:19). It was a greeting spoken over and over again in that society: "*Shalom aleichim.*" But now, after the "It is finished" of the cross, the "Peace be with you" takes on a different meaning. Now, because the Savior has been crucified for our sins, for our idolatry, for our fears, He speaks, "Peace be with you!" It is the same peace He gave out before His crucifixion: "My peace I give to you. Not as the world gives do I give to you" (John 14:27) and "In the world you will have tribulation. But take heart; I have overcome the world" (John 16:33). Now they see His overcoming. They see His nail-scarred hands and feet. They see His spear-pierced side. They begin to see that the price has been paid, that the sacrifice has been made, that nothing dare separate them from the Father.

The same is true for you. The dear Savior comes through locked doors still. He comes to hearts long locked with fear and brings His peace. Peace amidst the world's trials and struggles. Peace of ultimate dimensions. Peace of the forgiveness of sins. That is what Jesus speaks next. He breathed on them and said, "Receive the Holy Spirit. If you forgive the sins of any, they are forgiven them; if you withhold forgiveness from any, it is withheld" (John 20:22–23). What Jesus did has set things right between you and your Father.

In your Baptism, the Holy Spirit came to you and brought you to faith. In the Word of God, the Holy Spirit comes to you and strengthens your faith. In the Sacrament of the Altar, God the Holy Spirit strengthens your faith in this Crucified One, who is risen from the dead to give you the pledge and seal of forgiveness through His very body and blood. This is all Jesus breathing on you and saying, "Receive the Holy Spirit!"

All of this is possible only because our God has scars. His nail-pierced hands and feet and His spear-pierced side show us that He has paid the price. He has taken all our sins upon Himself. He has put them so deep into His scars that they never dare trouble us again. He has removed them from us, as far as the east is from the west (see Psalm 103:12). This is no whistling in the dark; this is no unfounded hope; this is no utopian dream. This hope is as real as Jesus' wounds.

Thomas came to know it too. "My Lord and my God!" he cried (John 20:28). Although we do not see Jesus now, we have been blessed with the sight of faith, the sight that sees Him coming through the locked doors of our hearts, breaking down the barriers, and saying, "Peace be with you!" You are forgiven! Thanks be to God.

Endnotes

1 Jonathan Rauch, "Let It Be: Three Cheers for Apatheism," *Articles by Jonathan Rauch* (blog) and *The Atlantic*, May 2003, https://jonathanrauch.typepad.com/jrauch_articles/apatheism_beyond_religion/index.html.

2 SC II (*LSCE*, p. 17).

3 Edward Shillito, "Jesus of the Scars," in *Christ in Poetry: An Anthology*, ed. Thomas Curtis Clark and Hazel Davis Clark (New York: Association, 1952), 137.

PARABLES OF THE RESURRECTION

John C. Wohlrabe Jr.

EACH Lord's Day, Christians confess: "I believe in . . . the resurrection of the body, and the life everlasting" (Apostles' Creed) or "I look for the resurrection of the dead and the life of the world to come" (Nicene Creed). So also, our Lutheran Confessions hold:

> Our churches teach that at the end of the world Christ will appear for judgment and will raise all the dead [1 Thessalonians 4:13–5:2]. He will give the godly and elect eternal life and everlasting joys, but He will condemn ungodly people and the devils to be tormented without end [Matthew 25:31–46]. (AC XVII 1–3)

Our Lord regularly proclaimed this truth during His earthly ministry, not only using direct discourse but also illustrating it through parables.

Approximately one third of the teachings of Jesus consist of parables. These stories or analogies describe something about what happens when God reestablishes Himself as King over His human creation.[1] The number of Jesus' parables ranges from thirty to seventy-nine, depending on who is counting.[2] For, you see, there is no clear and universally accepted definition of what constitutes a parable.[3] Some are specifically identified as such with the Greek word *parabole*, while others are not. Some parables recorded in the Synoptic Gospels are very similar yet vary on certain points, which means that Jesus probably told related yet differing parables during His ministry. When interpreting parables, the points of comparison are not meant to be complete in every detail, and not all points of the story are part of the comparison. Therefore, parables are not used to establish doctrine but to support ideas that are taught elsewhere in Scripture. Their purpose is to illustrate and reinforce biblical teaching. One should be open to observing both major and minor themes in parables.[4]

Two important points characteristic of the kingdom of God are articulated by Jesus in parables. First, the kingdom of God is to be understood in terms of God's grace. Second, the parables show that God chooses to dwell among His people to restore His reign among them.[5] God is active in reestablishing His kingdom in the midst of human beings by coming among them and graciously forgiving their sins through the reconciliation accomplished by the God-man, Jesus Christ, in His life, death, and resurrection. Obedience to God's reign involves the response of faith, receiving God's gracious invitation and Gospel gifts.[6]

Out of all the recorded parables of Jesus, I identified sixteen that relate to the resurrection either directly or indirectly. These parables are illustrative of what Scripture teaches elsewhere and can be divided into four general categories based on central truths within these accounts. From there, other minor observations relating to the resurrection can also be gleaned.

1. Patience: It Will Be Sorted Out at the Resurrection

The first two resurrection parables appear close together in Matthew's Gospel: the wheat and the weeds (Matthew 13:24–30, 36–43) and the dragnet (Matthew 13:47–50). Jesus provides the interpretation of both parables Himself.

The sower in the first parable (Matthew 13:24–30) is Jesus; the field is the world; the good seed that develops into wheat are the sons of the kingdom. The weeds—likely to be understood as bearded darnel, which looks similar to wheat—are sons of the evil one sown by the devil. The harvest is the Last Day (the close of the age), and the reapers are God's angels. Jesus does not directly explain who the servants are who would want to pull up the weeds with the wheat, but they may well be referring to the apostles or those directly tasked with caring for the Lord's fields before the harvest—namely, those in the office of the ministry. They are to leave things as they are and patiently await the harvest on the Last Day. Then God's angels will sort out the wheat from the weeds. The weeds, the sons of the evil one, will be cast into the fiery furnace, where there will be weeping and gnashing of teeth. Such weeping and gnashing most likely indicates continued hatred and rage toward God, similar to those who stoned Stephen in Acts 7:54, gnashing their teeth during his martyrdom. The sons of the kingdom will shine like the sun in God's heavenly kingdom.

The second of these parables, the dragnet (Matthew 13:47–50), compares the kingdom of heaven to a large net that brings in all sorts of sea life. But it is not sorted out until the net is full and brought ashore, where the fishermen separate the good from the bad. So it will be on the Last Day when the angels divide the evil from the righteous. The evil will be cast into the fiery furnace, where there will be weeping and gnashing of teeth.

In addition to directly pointing to the Last Day when the living and the dead are resurrected, and angels separate the sons of the kingdom who have faith in Jesus Christ from the sons of the evil one who reject Christ and His salvation, these parables offer a glimpse of the nature of heaven and hell. In heaven the sons of the kingdom will shine like the sun in the Lord's glorious presence. On the other hand, sons of the evil one will be cast into a place like a fiery furnace, where there will be suffering and ongoing hatred toward God.

2. Our Place in the Resurrection Rests on God's Gracious Invitation of Forgiveness

This section of Scripture includes five of Jesus' parables: the unforgiving servant (Matthew 18:23–35), the laborers in the vineyard (Matthew 20:1–16), the wedding feast in Matthew (22:1–14), the wedding feast in Luke (14:7–11), and the great banquet (Luke 14:12–24). The first two do not seem to have much in common with the last three, yet all involve God's grace.

The story of the unforgiving servant (Matthew 18:23–35) highlights God's generous forgiveness of our many sins, whether we receive this in grateful faith and then show it to others or not. A servant is forgiven an incredible debt by his master, more than a person could ever hope to repay. That servant then refuses to forgive a fellow servant who owes him a pittance. When the master hears of this, he has the unmerciful servant imprisoned until the impossible debt is repaid. Jesus concludes by saying that the heavenly Father will do the same to us if we do not forgive our brother from the heart. Refusal to forgive as one is generously forgiven by God demonstrates nonexistent faith. This parable alludes to the resurrection only indirectly, with eternal punishment being the consequence for those who have not gratefully grasped and appreciated the forgiveness of a merciful God by then showing mercy and forgiveness to others.

The parable of the laborers in the vineyard (Matthew 20:1–16) provides another indirect reference to the resurrection based on a gracious invitation to work in the master's vineyard. The point of this allegory is that the kingdom is given equally to all who are graciously called, regardless of the length of service involved during their earthly life.

The final three accounts in this section deal with gracious invitations to elaborate meals. The parable of the wedding feast (Matthew 22:1–14) involves a king (God the Father) who has invited his subjects to the wedding feast (heavenly banquet) of his son (Jesus, the Bridegroom). The king sends his servants (the prophets) to call those who were invited to come, but some made excuses, others ignored the invitation, and some even killed the servant messengers. Those who refused the invitation are judged with destruction. These first invitees correspond to the Jews, who were specifically chosen but then rejected the messianic invitation promised and fulfilled in Jesus the Christ. The king then sent out his servants to invite as many as they could find. God's invitation in Christ is for all people. Still, there was an individual who would not wear the wedding garment provided. He is cast out where, again, there is weeping and gnashing of teeth. The wedding garment is the righteousness of Christ that is ours through faith. Those who dishonor the King's Son by rejecting His invitation to the heavenly banquet or who think they have a place based on their own filthy, sinful garments will be cast out of the heavenly banquet, joining those who gnash their teeth against God in hatred. This parable ends with "For many are called, but few are chosen" (Matthew 22:14), which can be seen as a reference to God's election to grace through Jesus Christ (Romans 8:28–30; Ephesians 1:3–10).

The parable of the great banquet (Luke 14:15–24) is similar but with differences. First, in this story a man throws a great banquet. When the host sends his servants to call people to the banquet, they are confronted with excuses. So the host sends his servants to invite anyone and everyone, including the poor, the crippled, the blind, and the lame. This parable points indirectly to the resurrection, which is compared to a great banquet for those who receive the invitation and by God's grace attend, while those who refuse the invitation are excluded. Within the context of Luke 14, Jesus was invited to a banquet Himself and used this to instruct the host about not only inviting those who can reciprocate but also generously including the poor, the crippled, the lame, and the blind who cannot repay (Luke 14:12–14).

Just as the parable of the great banquet had an immediate application within the context, so does the parable of the wedding feast in Luke (14:7–11). Whereas the great banquet was pointed toward the host, the wedding feast is directed to the guests. When invited to a wedding reception, do not first sit in a place of honor, lest someone more important come and you are asked to move to an inferior place. Rather, sit in a lowly seat, and the host will then honor you by asking you to move up. Here we have more than practical advice on how to avoid embarrassment in public. In view of the other wedding feast/banquet parables, we enter the heavenly wedding feast in humility, repentance, and gratitude, trusting in God's grace through Jesus Christ and not in our own status. By God's grace in Christ, at the resurrection we will be elevated in the presence of almighty God and the heavenly hosts.

3. We Don't Know When—So Be Resurrection Ready!

Five parables point to the fact that we don't know when Christ will return to resurrect and judge. Therefore, we are advised to be ready. This includes several parables about a master who leaves his servants in charge, and the servants do not know when the master will return (Matthew 24:45–51; Mark 13:32–37; Luke 12:35–40; 12:42–48), as well as the story of the ten virgins/wedding attendants (Matthew 25:1–13).

Two of these parables address both wise and wicked servants (Matthew 24:45–51; Luke 12:42–48). In Matthew, the wise servant is found to be doing what the master asked when he returns and is blessed by being set over all his possessions. The wicked servant is drunk and beating fellow servants while the master is delayed. When the master returns unexpectedly, according to Matthew's account, the wicked servant is cut in pieces and placed with the hypocrites, where there is weeping and gnashing of teeth. In Luke, the wicked servant is placed with "the unfaithful," where he receives a beating. If the servant's acts were deliberate, then the beating is severe; if his actions were negligent, then the beating is light. In view of the guidance given on interpreting parables at the beginning of this essay, it is imprudent to draw definitive conclusions about degrees of punishment in hell from the parable in Luke, though it does seem to be an implication.

Two other parables address a man either going on a journey (Mark 13:32–37) or to a wedding feast (Luke 12:35–40). In both, he has placed servants in charge to remain awake and open the door when he returns. Those whom the master finds awake when he returns will be blessed. Because we do not know when Christ will return, we are to be awake and watchful in fervent faith.

The fifth parable in the "be ready" category is that of the ten virgins/wedding attendants (Matthew 25:1–13). In waiting for the coming of the bridegroom, five attendants were foolish and lacked sufficient oil for their lamps, whereas five were wise and had enough. When word arrived that the bridegroom was coming, the foolish asked the wise attendants to share their oil. The wise refused because there was not enough for them all. The foolish attendants were told to go out and buy some for themselves. While they were away to procure more oil, the bridegroom came. The five attendants with enough oil entered the wedding feast while the five foolish attendants were locked out and told by the bridegroom that he does not know them. The bridegroom is Jesus. There will be an interval of time until the Son's return in glory. The ten attendants represent the community of those who claim Christ as Lord—the visible church. The oil represents those things necessary to be ready: repentance, humble faith, use of the means of grace, and perseverance.

In all these parables, the admonition to watch and be ready predominates. Although we do not know when, there will be a resurrection, and those who are prepared in faith will be blessed, while those who are not prepared because of unbelief will be eternally excluded and face punishment.

4. Awaiting the Resurrection, We Trust God and His Word by Using the Gifts He Provides

Within this last section of parables on the resurrection, we find that two are similar and two others are quite unique. In fact, the latter two are so different that some are reluctant to classify them as parables. They are unique because they are not analogies; rather, they are pictures of what will happen.

The two similar stories are the parable of the talents (Matthew 25:14–30) and the parable of the ten minas (Luke 19:11–37). In Matthew's account, a man goes on a journey and entrusts his servants with his property. To one he gives five talents; to another, two talents; and to a third, one talent. A talent is equivalent to approximately twenty years' worth of salary.[7] Two of the servants, the one with five talents and the one with two talents, invest what was entrusted and double the master's property. The third buries the talent given to him and does nothing with it because he only fears the master. The master is Jesus Himself. His disciples are bought with a price and given new life to trust their Lord and use His Gospel gifts. The servant who did not trust his master is sent into outer darkness, where there is weeping and gnashing of teeth.

Luke's account is similar but different. Here, a nobleman is going away to a far country to receive a kingdom. He gives to ten of his servants ten minas, one mina each, and tells them to engage in business. A mina is about three months' wages.[8] Meanwhile, a delegation of citizens was sent to say that they did not want the nobleman as their king. When the nobleman returned, one servant came forward and said that his mina had earned ten minas. He is praised and rewarded by being placed over ten cities. Another servant came forward and said that his mina had earned five minas. He, too, is praised and rewarded by being placed over five cities. Another servant came forward and returned the mina, saying he laid it away in a handkerchief, for he feared the nobleman for being severe. Like the servant who buried the talent, he is reprimanded for not investing the mina. Here the mina is taken away and given to the one who had ten minas. Then the citizens who did not want the nobleman to reign over them are brought forward and slaughtered. Like the parable of the talents, the parable of the minas refers to Jesus' return on Judgment Day. He is the nobleman who entrusts us with gifts, particularly the gifts of salvation, faith, and His Word and Sacraments. We are to trust Him and put these gifts to use in our lives and the lives of others. By grace, He will bless those who use His gifts in faith. Those who do not trust His benevolence and reject His reign will face punishment on that final day.

The first of the two unique parables is the account of our Lord's coming in glory with all the angels on the Last Day (Matthew 25:31–46). It is not a parable in the usual sense because it is a direct teaching about what will happen. The nations, all people of all time, will be gathered before Christ, and He will separate the people as a shepherd separates sheep from goats. The sheep will be sent into the kingdom prepared for them from the foundation of the world, also described as eternal life, while the goats will be cast into the eternal fire prepared for the devil and his evil angels, referred to as eternal punishment. At first glance, the separation seems to be based on how well one cares for others in need. But it is important to understand exactly what Jesus is saying here: "As you did it to one of the least of these My brothers, you did it to Me" (Matthew 25:40). "Brother" here refers to Jesus' disciples (as is the case throughout Matthew's Gospel), those who have been sent out with the task of spreading the Gospel. Offering aid and hospitality to a messenger indicates that you believe the Gospel message.[9]

The other unique parable is the rich man and Lazarus (Luke 16:19–31). This also seems more of a direct teaching than an allegorical analogy. Here we have a glimpse of what heaven and hell are like. But the parable is not primarily about the joys of heaven or the horrors of hell, nor is its principle focus the dangers of wealth or the nobility of poverty. When the rich man (traditionally referred to as "Dives") asks that a messenger from the dead be sent to warn his brothers, father Abraham says, "They have Moses and the Prophets; let them hear them" (Luke 16:29). It was not riches that brought the rich man to hell, and it was not poverty that brought Lazarus to heaven; rather, Lazarus heard and believed the Word of God while the rich man did not. Moses and the prophets, or the Old Testament, point to the coming Messiah, from the promise of Genesis 3:15 to the blessing to all nations that would come from the offspring of Abraham, Isaac, and Jacob. This coming Messiah would come from the royal line of David and establish an eternal kingdom for those who believe. He who has ears to hear, let him hear and believe.

The resurrection parables of Jesus point to His second coming, at which time He will raise the living and the dead. In the meantime, we live in patient faith, trusting our Lord's Gospel promises. It will all be sorted out at the resurrection. Our place at the resurrection is secure because it rests on God's gracious invitation of forgiveness through Jesus Christ. We do not know when Jesus will return, so in the meantime we are to be ready by trusting in Christ, our Savior. As we await the resurrection, we make use of the Gospel gifts He provides.

Endnotes

1 Martin Scharlemann, *Proclaiming the Parables* (St. Louis: Concordia Publishing House, 1963), 13.

2 Scharlemann, *Proclaiming the Parables*, 18–19.

3 See Jefferey A. Gibbs, *Matthew 11:2–20:34*, Concordia Commentary (St. Louis: Concordia Publishing House, 2010), 665–68.

4 Scharlemann, *Proclaiming the Parables*, 30; Gibbs, *Matthew 11:2–20:34*, 660, 667.

5 Scharlemann, *Proclaiming the Parables*, 30.

6 Scharlemann, *Proclaiming the Parables*, 61.

7 See Gibbs, *Matthew 11:2–20:34*, 1331.

8 See Arthur A. Just Jr., *Luke 9:51–24:53*, Concordia Commentary (St. Louis: Concordia Publishing House, 1997), 726.

9 See Gibbs, *Matthew 11:2–20:34*, 1348, 1353–59.

RESURRECTION IN THE OLD TESTAMENT

Timothy J. Scharr

Your dead shall live; their bodies shall rise. You who dwell in the dust, awake and sing for joy! For your dew is a dew of light, and the earth will give birth to the dead. (Isaiah 26:19)

THE resurrection from the dead is a cardinal teaching of the Christian faith. St. Paul reminds the Corinthians of the centrality of the Gospel: "For I delivered to you as of first importance what I also received: that Christ died for our sins in accordance with the Scriptures, that He was buried, that He was raised on the third day in accordance with the Scriptures" (1 Corinthians 15:3–4). Indeed, Paul goes on to say that if Christ has not been raised from the dead, then our preaching and your faith are in vain (1 Corinthians 15:14). Everything hinges on Jesus rising from the dead (1 Corinthians 15:14–19).

Resurrection from the dead is not only a New Testament teaching. Paul carefully cites that Christ's death, burial, and resurrection were in accordance with the Scriptures. As Paul wrote, the clearly recognized Scripture was the Old Testament. The New Testament books were still being written and compiled. It was from the Old Testament that Paul asserts the primacy of the crucifixion, burial, and resurrection from the dead. Jesus fulfills what had long been promised: "Your dead shall live; their bodies shall rise" (Isaiah 26:19).

The triune God is the author of life and creation. God forms the universe and all that is seen and unseen by the breath of His Word (Psalm 33:6). The Lord formed Adam from dust of the ground and breathed into his nostrils the breath of life (Genesis 2:7). God placed the man in the garden, but no suitable helper was found. The Lord caused deep sleep to fall upon the man. From the man's rib the Lord built Eve in the garden and gave her to the man (Genesis 2:21–23). Life abounded as the Lord gave every green plant for food to man and beast alike. God saw it all, and it was very good (Genesis 1:31).

Death was unknown before the fall into sin (Genesis 3). The Lord God warned Adam not to eat the fruit from one tree, the tree of the knowledge of good and evil. In the day that he would eat from that tree, death would come into the world, and he would surely die. Satan, in the guise of a serpent, tempted Eve with the desirability of the fruit from the forbidden tree. He twisted what God had said to Adam so that Eve would question what God had told her through her husband. Worse yet, Adam was with her and did not silence the serpent and correct the error that was presented. The couple ate, and immediately their eyes were opened. Sin filled them within and from without. They were ashamed of their nakedness. They hid from God as they heard His presence in the garden. Things would never be the same.

The temporary coverings that Adam and Eve fashioned for themselves from fig leaves proved inadequate. God killed the first animals to make clothes of animal skins for their bodies (Genesis 3:21). This simple act foreshadowed the substitution God would make to repair His fallen creation and restore it to Himself. The Seed of the woman would come. This Seed would suffer a mortal wound to the heel but in the process would crush the skull of the serpent (Genesis 3:15).

Death was now part of creation. The ground was cursed because of Adam. Work became toil. Childbirth would be painful from this time forward. Women would desire to rule the household, but God maintained the headship with the man. Most of all, creation was divided, and people were separated from God. The death of the first human was only a matter of time.

Martin Luther captured the joy and expectation that Adam and Eve placed upon their firstborn son, Cain. They were overjoyed to see this seed of the woman come to fruition. They saw Cain as the fulfillment of the protoevangelium (Genesis 3:15). Imagine their horror when their firstborn becomes the first murderer by taking the life of his brother, Abel. Abel's death foreshadows life after physical death. The Lord confronts Cain: "What have you done? The voice of your brother's blood is crying to Me from the ground" (Genesis 4:10). Blood speaking from the ground implies a continuation of life beyond death. The Lenten hymn captures it well: "Abel's blood for vengeance pleaded to the skies; but the blood of Jesus for our pardon cries" (*LSB* 433:4).

If death had never entered the world, would every living creature remain on the earth eternally? Death was not in the Lord's design for creation. The accounts of Enoch (Genesis 5:21–24) and Elijah (2 Kings 2:9–12a) may shed light. At some point, the Lord may have taken people out of this life to His nearer presence, as He did with Enoch and Elijah. Or, considering that the world was created "very good," the whole earth was habitable and fruitful from pole to pole. Under the permafrost in the Baffin Islands of northern Canada, stumps from tropical trees have been discovered. These trees are found only in equatorial zones today. A sinless, temperate, bountiful, fruitful earth without deserts or wilderness or uninhabitable places could easily accommodate far more people than many can imagine. The dwelling of God would remain with men just as God walked with Adam and Eve in the cool of the day in the garden (Genesis 3:8). Without sin and death, there would be no reason to hide from the Lord's presence.

It is interesting that in the beginning all creation was very good. Yet there was a special place, the Garden of Eden, where God's nearer presence was celebrated. It was an elevated place, as from it flowed a river with four branches (Genesis 2:10). Eden also had boundaries. After sin entered the world, Adam and Eve were sent out of the garden. A cherub with flaming sword guarded against their return (Genesis 3:23–24). At the end of the Bible, in Revelation 21 and 22, the Lord creates a new heaven and a new earth, which is the home of righteousness. Like Eden, the new Jerusalem has definite boundaries and open gates. It comes down out of heaven from God. In the center of the city, there is a garden where the tree of life grows alongside a river. It bears different fruits, year-round. This is the holy city with "foundations, whose designer and builder is God" (Hebrews 11:10). This is the better country, a heavenly one longed for by the patriarchs of old (Hebrews 11:16). Isaiah notes that upon this mountain:

> The Lord of hosts will make for all peoples a feast of rich food, a feast of well-aged wine, of rich food full of marrow, of aged wine well refined. . . . He will swallow up death forever; and the Lord God will wipe away tears from all faces, and the reproach of His people He will take away from all the earth, for the Lord has spoken. It will be said on that day, "Behold, this is our God; we have waited for Him, that He might save us. This is the Lord; we have waited for Him; let us be glad and rejoice in His salvation." (Isaiah 25:6–9)

Sin, death, resurrection, and restoration are the perennial themes of the prophets. When the Messiah comes, He will make all things new. The fulfillment, however, will be lived in its completeness, eternally, after the Last Day. Then the dwelling of God will be with men. Ezekiel writes: "They shall not defile themselves anymore with their idols and their detestable things, or with any of their transgressions. But I will save them from all the backslidings in which they have sinned, and will cleanse them; and they shall be My people, and I will be their God" (Ezekiel 37:23).

In Genesis 22, we have the account of Abraham following God's command to sacrifice his son Isaac. Abraham and Isaac left the two young men behind as they went up to the mountain. Abraham told them that he and the boy would go over there and worship and come again to them (Genesis 22:5). As they went along, Isaac asked about the sacrifice they were to make. Abraham told him that the Lord would provide for Himself the lamb for a burnt offering. At this point, Abraham did not know exactly what would happen with Isaac. The New Testament provides divine commentary: "[Abraham] considered that God was able even to raise him from the dead, from which, figuratively speaking, he did receive him back" (Hebrews 11:19). The resurrection of the dead was believed by the father of God's Old Testament people.

Speaking from the burning bush, the Lord Himself taught Moses that the dead live. God identifies Himself as "I am the God of your father, the God of Abraham, the God of Isaac, and the God of Jacob" (Exodus 3:6). Note the present tense. The Lord God remains the God of these patriarchs. Even though they died, they yet live. Jesus confirms this: "He is not the God of the dead, but of the living" (Matthew 22:32).

The prophet Elijah and his successor, Elisha, were literally used by the Lord to raise the dead. As Elijah fled from the wrath of King Ahab, he sought refuge in the home of a widow in Zarephath. The son of the widow became sick and died. The widow blamed this misfortune on the prophet living in her home. The prophet took the boy into his room and laid him on the bed. He stretched himself on the child three times and cried out to the Lord, pleading that God would let life come into the child again. The Lord listened to Elijah, and life returned to the boy. The prophet presented him to his mother. She said, "Now I know that you are a man of God, and that the word of the LORD in your mouth is truth" (1 Kings 17:24).

Elisha prophesied that a Shunammite would conceive a son though her husband was old. The boy was born. When he had grown, he went out among the reapers to see his father. He suffered a grievous head wound. The boy was carried to his mother; he lived a short time and then died. The woman made her way to Elisha at Mount Carmel. The mother would not leave Elisha until he returned with her. Finding the dead boy, Elisha prayed. As Elijah had done, Elisha stretched out upon the child, face-to-face, mouth-to-mouth, and eye-to-eye. He placed his hands on the boy's hands. The flesh of the child became warm, and life returned to his body. The child sneezed seven times and opened his eyes. The Shunammite woman came in and picked up her son and went out—another resurrection from the dead by the Lord through His prophet Elisha (2 Kings 4:18–37).

The power of the resurrection is illustrated beautifully by Ezekiel through what he saw in the valley full of dry bones (Ezekiel 37). The Lord asked the prophet, "Can these bones live?" Ezekiel wisely answered, "O Lord GOD, You know" (Ezekiel 37:3). The Lord commanded Ezekiel to speak the word of the Lord over these bones. As the prophet prophesied, the bodies literally came back together! Bone to bone, sinews, flesh, and skin—but no breath in them. The Lord commanded Ezekiel to prophesy to the breath. From the four winds breath came upon these who were dead, and they lived! They comprised an "exceedingly great army" (Ezekiel 37:10).

God Himself interprets what Ezekiel saw. These bones are the whole house of Israel. The Lord will open their graves and raise them from the dead. God will put His Spirit within them, and they shall live. He will place them in their own land. Then they "shall know that I am the LORD; I have spoken, and I will do it, declares the LORD" (Ezekiel 37:14). This is the resurrection *according to the Scriptures* about which Paul wrote (see 1 Corinthians 15:3).

One of the brilliant Hebrew young men carried away from Jerusalem and into captivity in Babylon was Daniel. He served in the Babylonian court as one of the wise men of the empire and a ruler of the people. He was gifted by the Lord to interpret dreams. This was not an ordinary gift. The Lord enabled Daniel to tell the king both what he had dreamed and what it meant. No other man could do this. The humble, faithful Daniel grew in favor with the royal court. The Lord chose to reveal the future to him through a series of visions. One vision spoke of the end times and of the resurrection of all flesh: "But at that time your people shall be delivered, everyone whose name shall be found written in the book. And many of those who sleep in the dust of the earth shall awake, some to everlasting life, and some to shame and everlasting contempt" (Daniel 12:1–2). It is a common feature of Hebrew grammar to use "many" when "all" is implied. Jesus employs this in Matthew 20:28 when He promises to give His life as a "ransom for many." The analogy of faith shows that "He died for all" (2 Corinthians 5:15). Daniel clearly teaches the resurrection from the dead on the Last Day.

Perhaps the clearest confession of the resurrection for the individual believer comes from the lips of Job. This long-suffering, beleaguered believer was tormented by the friends who came to console him. Job finally had had enough. He longed that his words be written down, engraved in rock forever. They live in every printed Bible. Job knew that death awaited him. He knew that his body would decay in the ground. He confidently confessed his faith in the Lord. Job was a contemporary of Abraham. Some two thousand years before the Messiah appeared in human flesh, Job asserted that his close kinsman, his Redeemer, lives. He further confessed that his Redeemer would be alive and on the earth on Judgment Day. Job will also be there. He will have a resurrected and glorified body. The very body that he was watching decay and die before him would go the way of all flesh but later be resurrected. He says, "And after my skin has been thus destroyed, yet in my flesh I shall see God, whom I shall see for myself, and my eyes shall behold, and not another" (Job 19:26–27). Note the intensity of his confession and the repetition of the first-person pronoun: *my* skin destroyed, yet in *my* flesh, *I* shall see God, *I* shall see for *myself*, and *my* eyes shall behold, and not another. Job boldly asserted that his very own eyes would be resurrected and see the world's only Redeemer. Job could hardly wait for this day. We share the same resurrection hope in Jesus Christ. Every Easter the Holy Christian Church sings Job's words and confesses the faith in the hymn "I Know That My Redeemer Lives" (*LSB* 461).

From this brief survey, we see that Paul accurately wrote of the resurrection according to the Scriptures (1 Corinthians 15:3), the Old Testament. Both Testaments affirm this same teaching. The dead live now. Their souls are either with Christ or in hell. The bodies that are laid to rest decay. At the end, they will be raised and reunited with their souls—some to everlasting life, some to everlasting contempt, but live they will. These eyes—my eyes, your eyes—risen and glorified, will see it. With Job we cry out: "My heart yearns within me!" (Job 19:27 NKJV).

GOD'S NEON SIGN

The raising of Lazarus, about two weeks or so before Jesus' own death, has been called an "acted out parable." It is like a huge neon sign with a big arrow—"Look this way!"—pointing to Jesus' own resurrection from the dead.

Rev. Dr. Herbert C. Mueller Jr.

NEON SIGNS OF THE RESURRECTION

The Widow's Son, Jairus's Daughter, and Lazarus

Steven C. Theiss

HAVE you ever experienced something so exciting, so wonderfully uplifting, that you simply could not stop talking about it? For those who share this great joy with you, the message bears repeating. The birth of a child or a first grandchild usually produces this kind of joy. It often beams on the face of the thrilled parents or grandparents even before they reach you. It is almost like a neon sign, shining brightly through their eyes and smile. In some cultures, the message is made into a song or conveyed from one person to another with gestures and dance. That kind of good news can spread like wildfire. It lights up the faces and the minds of those who hear it, and they keep passing the news to others. When was the last time you encountered such great news?

Jesus performed multiple miracles in the full sight of many people. Some of the people present at those miracles were disciples. Some were curious followers. Still others were completely opposed to Jesus and His actions. Those opposed to Jesus sometimes tried to explain away His miracles. "He casts out demons by Beelzebul" was offered (Luke 11:15). They could and would simply discount what others told them. They also made attacks on the character or the reliability of those bringing the message. But not all the resurrection events can be so easily rejected, let alone refuted. Jesus' miracles of resurrection shine brightly, like neon signs.

The Widow's Son at Nain (Luke 7:11–17)

Luke 7:11–17 describes the meeting of two groups. "A great crowd" was accompanying Jesus and His disciples as they neared the city of Nain. (Nain lies about nine miles southeast of Nazareth.) At that same time, a funeral procession was exiting the city. A sizable crowd was escorting the funeral party, most likely headed for the many tombs to the east of Nain. It was at this meeting of the crowds that the bright light of God's power over death broke through "the shadow of death" (Psalm 23:4).

Every parent knows that it can happen. Yet none of us really expect it. The parent, the elder, is expected to die first, then the younger person. But clearly, quite visibly, as the bier was carried out through the entrance to the city, the tragedy was real. Death plunged its ugly presence once again into the home and the heart of this widow. In Nain the mother was alone. Her husband was no longer alive. He could not support her in this terrible time. He was not present to give comfort, to share the grief. Her loss was intense, the hurt numbing and penetrating.

Jesus is moved by this spectacle. Jesus acts. His first action is a word of comfort, an invitation to leave behind her grief. "Do not weep," says the one who numbers each of our days before one of them comes to be (Luke 7:13). She cannot know why, but soon the actions of the Lord Jesus will shine truth into her empty, dark, and broken spirit. The God of the widow stands in the way of death. He stops the walk of woe that this widow thought would end at the burial site that day.

The widow's only child, a son, had so recently died, yet this day would certainly turn out differently than she had expected. We are not told, but most likely the young man had not been dead more than one day. It is even possible that this only son had died that very morning. He who is the God of the widow, the God of the fatherless, will not permit death to reign in this place. The only-begotten Son of God, the firstborn of Mary, meets the needs of His people on life's road and turns the terrible into the amazing. He turns sorrow into joy, tears into laughter, and death into life.

For the crowds following Jesus and the mourners accompanying this widow of Nain, the Light of the world breaks the darkness of death. The firstborn Son of Mary, the only-begotten Son of God, raises an only son from death. This would not be the last time He does so.

Jesus still reaches out to touch. He does not hesitate to touch the unclean. He reaches for the untouchable ones to remove the pall, the shroud of death, that covers the face of the world. At Nain, Jesus first stops death's advance, and then He speaks life into the young man. The dead one hears the voice of his God and lives! What is more, the young man speaks. All those present, a great crowd, see and hear. The dead one is now alive. The silence of death is penetrated by the Word of life, and the living speak out.

The Daughter of Jairus (Luke 8:40–42, 49–56)

Jesus performed some miracles in private, with only disciples or family members in attendance. The raising of the daughter of Jairus was one of those miracles. At the request of this father, Jesus heads for Jairus's house. Jesus did not agree to go with him because of this man's position in the synagogue but because of the faith evident in his appeal. The light seems to go out as they walk to that house. Word comes that the daughter has died. Our Lord is clear that death will not deter Him. Once again, the Good Shepherd speaks comfort: "Do not fear; only believe, and she will be well" (Luke 8:50); "Do not weep, for she is not dead but sleeping" (Luke 8:52).

See again how our Savior brings comfort in times of hurt. Jesus speaks faith into His loved ones in the face of fear. He knows our sorrows and perceives our weakness in the face of death. But the one who holds the keys will not let death swallow up those who trust in Him. He has come to do the swallowing up, and death cannot escape.

Jesus always seeks to build up those who follow Him. He leaves outside those who laugh in scorn at His words and doubt His statement. They do not witness this miracle. Only the parents and the "inner circle" of Peter, John, and James are allowed in the house with Jesus. We can imagine the tears of joy when the twelve-year-old young lady sits up, alive! And the proof of life restored is the act of eating food, swallowing up the source of strength for physical life.

Yet Jesus says to keep this miracle under wraps; it is not to be discussed outside of the house. He does not explain why, though we may guess. To whom will our risen Lord appear after death? Not those who laughed in scorn but to those who wept in sorrow.

Jesus reaches out to touch. Jesus speaks words that bring life. At Nain, in the home of Jairus, and at Bethany, the Lord of creation makes it crystal clear that death has no authority over Him. To this day Jesus does not hesitate to touch our corruption, for it is fully under His power.

Lazarus (John 11:1–44)

Jesus' opponents included the scribes, Pharisees, Sadducees, and religious leaders of Judea. When it came to the miracles Jesus worked, they wanted to keep people in the dark. Jesus lamented their hardness of heart. He condemned their lack of faith and their misleading of those they taught. He reproved them because they both misused and failed to use properly the written words of the prophets or the Torah. Jesus clearly desired all people to receive the truth. Ultimately, Jesus acted to prove He was who He claimed to be.

Jesus receives word that His friend Lazarus is sick, deathly ill. He does not hasten to help. He hunkers down and bides *His* time. He waits because this matter had to be dealt with in God's own time. God moves when He decides the moment is right. ("When the fullness of time had come, God sent forth His Son, born of woman," Galatians 4:4.) So Jesus stays away long enough for the light to go out from the eyes of Lazarus.

Then He tells His disciples that the right moment had come. They do not perceive what Jesus is doing. Once again, Jesus states that Lazarus, like the twelve-year-old girl, is sleeping. We who walk in this world so often do not perceive the hidden work of God. He knows, but He will not always explain things to us. Our Rescuer still calls us to walk in the light that His Word casts on our path. Martha walks that lighted path. She trusts that Jesus can do what no other could do. She knows God will give Jesus whatever He would ask. She cannot keep this good news in silence. Faith speaks its hope.

When Jesus does arrive in Bethany, people notice. What Jesus was there to do would be done in full view of all those who mourned. God does not always hide the miracle. At times, as repeatedly recorded in the Bible, God shines light into the darkness. In the wilderness, the pillar of cloud by day and the pillar of fire by night were constantly visible to all the Israelites (see Exodus 13:22). It was never out of sight. That fact, in time, led to a common human reaction. Our self-centered sinful flesh fails to observe the sign God has given. We see rainbows in the sky as light is refracted by water vapor, but we often forget it is God's sign of promise (see Genesis 9:12–17). Familiarity leads to apathy before it becomes contempt.

Arriving in the hometown of Lazarus, who was four-days dead at that point, Jesus again speaks His word of promise. Martha believes a future resurrection is certain, at an unknown date. Still, her words to Jesus about her brother's decaying body reflect our own rational approach to the issue of dying. It is inevitable for us, irreversible for us, but not so for Jesus. At times, the Lord Christ wills otherwise.

The Lord of this world does much more than weep at death. He turns on the bright neon sign of life, for He is going to the place of burial (unlike the event at Nain, when nobody and *no body* reached the tombs). Sorrow at death, at the corruption of human nature by sin, at the fact that His friend did die, shows the care our Good Shepherd holds for His sheep.

The place of burial and despair, the place where death is covered in strips of cloth and decay has been hidden inside a tomb, does not deter the Word who became flesh. "In Him was life, and the life was the light of men" (John 1:4). Jesus has come to turn on that light of life in times of darkness in our lives, just as He did at Bethany.

The Rock who is our salvation speaks to the living mourners and the crowd that has once again accompanied Him. "Take away the stone" (John 11:39). The stone could not move itself, though Jesus could have done that. Martha, still focused on the physical signs, speaks of the odor of death. Jesus is not bothered by this, for He knows that life is about to shine into the darkness. The darkness cannot grasp what the Light of Life is doing. Jesus cannot be stopped. "Did I not tell you that if you believed you would see the glory of God?" (John 11:40). The glory of God shines out from inside the cloud that obscures our vision. The Lord Jesus addresses the Father as together They work the divine purpose.

Jesus is about to flip the switch on the brightest miracle since the Word spoke " 'Let there be light,' and there was light" (Genesis 1:3). Now, the God who speaks things into existence speaks to the dead brother inside the tomb: "Lazarus, come out" (John 11:43). And Lazarus came out, alive, but still in need of help from outside himself. Jesus could have spoken the cloths loose, but He did not. Instead, He speaks to those around Him and to death itself: "Unbind him, and let him go" (John 11:44).

These parables of action point to the final victory that Jesus will accomplish after His own death. He dies for the sins of others, for the sins of all others, and conquers death for all others. His miracles were seen by a few, by many, and always by our enemies—sin, death, and the evil one.

Sadly, just as happened when the neon sign of life from the dead was illuminated almost two thousand years ago, the darkness still attacks the light. But the light shines in the dark places of our world, our times, our lives, and the darkness can never extinguish the Light of Life. Those opposed to Jesus—and thus opposed to God's plan for the one He sent—plotted. Not only was Jesus targeted, but also the proof of life, Lazarus, was to be done away with.

How foolish that idea seems to us now. If Jesus could raise Lazarus once, would killing Lazarus stop Jesus from what He was sent to accomplish? But the darkness has never comprehended the Light.

None of us know the day when our time on earth will come to an end. We may die at any moment, or Jesus may return at any moment. These things are not even known to the angels of heaven. But all of this is known to the Light of the world, and for as long as we live, He shines on us. By the work of the Holy Spirit, the Lord and Giver of life, that light shines through us into the darkness. Also, by the grace of God, others will see this great news of eternal life reflected from our faces.

TRUE TEACHING

THE EASTER EFFECT

"If Christ has not been raised . . ." (1 Corinthians 15:17)

Perhaps you have noticed, as I have, that, as the celebration of Easter approaches, there often appear in the secular media (*Time*, *Newsweek*, CNN, the History Channel, etc.) articles or programs designed to provide some kind of alternative explanation for the resurrection of Jesus. So when I came across "The Easter Effect," an article by the Roman Catholic scholar George Weigel in the Easter weekend edition of *The Wall Street Journal*, my initial reaction was on the order of "Here we go again!" But after reading the article, I was pleasantly surprised. The "Easter effect" is Weigel's term for the effect the resurrection of Jesus had on His initial followers and the early church. Weigel makes the case that what actually happened in the first hundred years after the crucifixion of Jesus can be explained *only* if Jesus truly did bodily rise from the grave.

What does he mean? Putting aside pious tradition, according to Weigel, Constantine the Great was making a shrewd political decision when, after winning the undisputed leadership of the Roman Empire at the Battle of the Milvan Bridge in AD 312, he promulgated the Edict of Milan in AD 313.

His pronouncement ended legal sanctions on the public profession of faith in Jesus Christ. Weigel says Constantine was just joining the winning side, since by his day about half the population was Christian and the numbers were still growing.

How did a ragtag bunch of nobodies from the eastern edge of the Mediterranean world become such a dominant force in only 250 years? Certainly Christians modeled a nobler way of life, bearing one another's burdens (Galatians 6:2), and this in stark contrast to the violence of their pagan surroundings. There was the compelling witness of the martyrs as well as the preaching of the cross and resurrection of Jesus. More than that, in an age of plagues, Weigel points out that Christians cared for anyone who fell sick, not only those in their own circles. Christians also had larger families because of their prohibition of abortion and infanticide.

But how did this modeling of an alternative lifestyle start in the first place? What happened to those early followers of Jesus after He was crucified? What happened to them is what Weigel terms "the Easter effect." The disciples met the risen Lord whom they had witnessed die on the cross. Because Jesus rose from the dead, the lives of these nobodies changed forever. The resurrection of Jesus turned upside down both their rhythm of time and the way they thought about worship. Despite coming from a Jewish background that notably observed the Sabbath (Saturday) as the day of rest and worship, a day chosen by God Himself, the early Christians worshiped on the "Lord's Day"—Sunday—because on this day Jesus rose from the dead.

Finally, was it delusion or denial that moved Christians to allow themselves, under persecution, to be marched off to execution? No, again Weigel puts forward as explanation "the Easter effect." They were fully convinced not only that Jesus had risen from the dead but that they also would rise to new life. It was "the joy of people who had become convinced that they were witnesses to something inexplicable but nonetheless true. Something that gave a superabundance of meaning to life and that erased the fear of death. Something that had to be shared. Something with which to change the world." In other words, the church grew because Jesus truly rose from the dead.

Rev. Dr. Herbert C. Mueller Jr.

THE RESURRECTION MAKES ALL THINGS NEW

Frederic W. Baue

IT'S so simple, really. "In the beginning, God created the heavens and the earth. . . . And God saw everything that He had made, and behold, it was very good" (Genesis 1:1, 31). The Apostles' Creed says, "I believe in God, the Father Almighty, maker of heaven and earth." The Nicene Creed adds "and of all things visible and invisible." Pastor Herb Mueller believed firmly in these things, referred to them in his notes, and intended to include a chapter on creation in his proposed book on the resurrection of our Lord. In this essay, I will briefly explore the doctrine of creation as it pertains to the resurrection in three parts: the first world, the present world, and the world to come.

The First World

Before bringing in the resurrection, we need to establish what the first world was like as God originally created it. We must try to see what the first world was like as a point of comparison with the present world and the world to come. Eden is closed to us now; the new earth has not yet opened. But we can comprehend the first world somewhat, for it contained things with which we are familiar in our present world: oceans, land, plants, fish, birds, animals, trees, rivers, and people. God called it "very good" (Genesis 1:31). Therefore, it seems reasonable to suppose that these things will be present also in the world to come, even as they are in the present world.

Perfect people in a perfect world. That was the condition of the first man and the first woman in the first world that God created *ex nihilo* ("out of nothing"), by the word of His mouth. Note, though, that the Greek word for "almighty" is *pantokrator*, from *pan*, "all," and *kratos*, "strength." It means not only that God made the world in the beginning but also that He still governs His created things. "And still takes care of them," as the Small Catechism says.[1]

The Lord made all things, visible and invisible. He made the angels, but Scripture does not say when. The angels were fixed in number, sentient beings of pure spirit, in their nature most like God. But whom should God create to be supreme upon earth but something quite unlike Himself: man, a sentient physical being in a material world, able to reproduce, not yet confirmed in holiness, though originally made in the image of God. The angels were likewise unconfirmed in holiness, for at some point there was war in heaven; Satan fell like lightning, and a third of the company of heaven with him. As a result, some angels were confirmed in unalterable goodness on the one hand, and others were confirmed in unalterable evil on the other. Man, therefore, was unique in this: he was able both to be lost and to be saved.

Let us not forget other invisible things. I am indebted to Dr. David Menton (1938–2021) of blessed memory for the insight that when God said, "Let there be light" (Genesis 1:3), He included everything on the electromagnetic spectrum, from the smallest gamma rays, X-rays, and ultraviolet rays; to visible light in the middle, followed by infrared and radar; to the largest FM, TV, shortwave, and AM waves. This includes not only light you can see but also light you can hear.[2]

Then there are the hidden forces, those mysterious things that guide birds in their migrations, fish in their spawning, and whales through the sea. Everything was *tsedek*—perfectly in alignment. The climate was just right, with plenty of water and fertile soil to grow good things. The planet on its axis, just the right distance from the sun.

Can we even begin to imagine the unsullied beauty and harmony of Adam and Eve before the fall? It was the first marriage, blessed by God. How pure was their love for each other, how radiant the presence of the Lord as He spoke with them face-to-face, how delicious the fruit from the trees and the herbs from the ground, how wonderful to live in peace with the animals.[3]

I tried to imagine it in one of my first books.[4] Of course, all I had to work with was the tarnished beauty of the fallen world into which I was born. Even in a fallen world, we read of super-talented people such as Mozart in music, Einstein in physics, Shakespeare in literature. What astounding mental and physical powers must Adam have had to name all the animals, plus all the other things he had to do in his dominion over all things. This, then, is the world that was.

The Present World

"It is very good," said God of the first world. It did not last. We ruined it, as we know all too well. But if man can be redeemed, the creation God made for him can be also. This will be resurrection power at work, and it is at work even in the world we inhabit today.

What, then, shall we say of the human race? The fourfold condition of man has been aptly described in a series of Latin aphorisms, said to derive from St. Augustine:

1. Before the fall: *Posse peccare, posse non peccare.* "Possible to sin, possible not to sin."
2. After the fall: *Non posse non peccare.* "Not possible not to sin."
3. By faith in Christ: *Posse non peccare.* "Possible not to sin."
4. In eternity: *Non posse peccare.* "Not possible to sin."

The first of these describes the spiritual condition of Adam. It is as if he were on probation, to see what he would do given free will and a choice. To me the most shocking thing about the temptation in the garden was that Adam was right there the whole time Eve was being beguiled by Satan: "She also gave some to her husband *who was with her*" (Genesis 3:6, emphasis added). He knew the serpent was lying. Eve was deceived; Adam was not. He knew it was wrong, but he did it anyway. That is why we call original sin the "old Adam," not the "old Eve." So all mankind lives *non posse non peccare*, except for the intrusion of Christ into this fallen world.

The third aphorism describes the spiritual condition of the Christian in the present world. Christ has intervened and taken away the sins of the world by His holy, innocent, bitter suffering and death on a cross. He has risen from the dead and ascended into heaven and taken His seat at the right hand of God. He and the Father have sent the Holy Spirit into the world. The saving Word is connected to the means of grace—Baptism and Communion.

Let's say a child has been brought to the eight-sided font and has been baptized and filled with the Holy Spirit. Now the state of that child is *posse non peccare*, "possible not to sin." Of course, sin taints everything we do. But as we are declared righteous for Christ's sake, so also our good works, inspired and empowered by the Holy Spirit, are acceptable to God as if Jesus Himself had done them. In this way they lay up treasure in heaven for us.

The resurrection changes everything. It changed the body of Jesus. He was still Jesus after He rose from the dead. He was not a ghost; He had flesh and bones. But He was different. Sometimes people did not recognize Him. Mary thought He was the gardener (John 20:15). Thomas had to see the wounds. The Emmaus disciples only recognized Him in the breaking of the bread (Luke 24:31). Walls were no obstacle to Him (John 20:19). He commanded the fish to fill the nets of the apostles (John 21:6), an echo of Adam, who had dominion even over the fish of the sea.

What of the world itself? This was made clear to Adam: "Cursed is the ground because of you; in pain you shall eat of it all the days of your life; thorns and thistles it shall bring forth for you. . . . By the sweat of your face you shall eat bread" (Genesis 3:17–19). This is the condition of the present world—earthquakes, floods, volcanic eruptions, these natural disasters properly called "acts of God." These are harbingers of the second coming of Christ.

St. Paul tells the Romans: "For the creation was subjected to futility, not willingly, but because of Him who subjected it, in hope that the creation itself will be set free from its bondage to corruption and obtain the freedom of the glory of the children of God. For we know that the whole creation has been groaning together in the pains of childbirth until now" (Romans 8:20–22). Here Paul speaks clearly not of the resurrection of the body, as in 1 Corinthians 15, but of the resurrection, if we can call it that, of creation itself.

Regarding the creation, sin changed everything for the worse, but the resurrection will change everything for the better. Jesus' resurrection was capped by His ascension into heaven and His session at the right hand of God. The angel told the apostles plainly: "This Jesus, who was taken up from you into heaven, will come in the same way as you saw Him go into heaven" (Acts 1:11). So we see from Scripture that the world had a beginning and will have an end.

The resurrection changes everything, even in this present world. Christ is seated at the right hand of God and rules and reigns over all things, visible and invisible, for all things were made through Him (John 1:1–3). He is *Pantokrator*. And His resurrection power is always at work in the church, through Baptism, through the Sacrament of the Altar, through Confession and Absolution, through Holy Scripture, through the Confessions, through liturgy, through prayers, through hymns, through music, through art and architecture, textiles and vestments, glass and glory.

The World to Come

We have seen that the resurrected Christ was like yet unlike the one we knew. His divine majesty, His omniscience, and His omnipotence were no longer concealed. We caught a glimpse of this at the Mount of Transfiguration

(Matthew 17:1–8). John also described it in Revelation 1. He saw Jesus in a glorified body. St. Paul spoke about this regarding our own future mode of living: "So it is with the resurrection of the dead. What is sown is perishable; what is raised is imperishable. It is sown in dishonor; it is raised in glory. It is sown in weakness; it is raised in power. It is sown a natural body; it is raised a spiritual body" (1 Corinthians 15:42–44). We will be physical people with material bodies, just as Jesus was after He rose again. But we will have bodies that cannot sin and cannot die. In the same way, creation also will be transformed, as St. Paul declares "that the creation itself will be set free from its bondage to corruption and obtain the freedom of the glory of the children of God" (Romans 8:21). That is to say, it will be like yet unlike the world we know.

One must of course tread lightly when interpreting the Revelation of St. John. Some things are literal; much is symbolic. For example, the seven churches of Asia Minor were all real places with real problems. "The dragon, that ancient serpent" in Revelation 20:2 is "the devil and Satan." The text explains the symbolism. The thousand years are symbolic. Ten is the number of completion (ten fingers, ten plagues, Ten Commandments), so the thousand years is 10 x 10 x 10, meaning a long time of indeterminate length. This is the present age of grace when the devil is bound so that the Gospel can be preached everywhere.

"Then," John says, "I saw a new heaven and a new earth, for the first heaven and the first earth had passed away, and the sea was no more" (Revelation 21:1). Is any of this literal? Christ has risen, ascended, been seated, returned to earth, and held the last judgment. That much we know is literal. He has cast the devil and death and Hades into the lake of fire. That sounds symbolic, though the metaphor conveys the idea that these evil things are in a place of everlasting punishment. For this new heaven and new earth, the Greek word *kaine* is used, "new in relation to the old," as in *New* Testament. No more sea? Symbolic. The sea, with its constant churning but fixed limits, represents history, the affairs of men. This image tells us that human history is over. The beast from the sea in Revelation 13, according to Dr. Louis Brighton, is the tyrannical power (governmental, social, economic, etc.) that attacks the church.[5] So it seems to me that the world God made and pronounced "very good" will find its futility (Romans 8:20) alleviated by the refining fire (2 Peter 3:10) which, like death for the human body, burns away sin and corruption.

In the world to come there will be things similar to the first world and the present world that we now live in: earth, air, water, trees, birds, fish, animals. And people—my parents, the grandparents I never knew, forebears who left Germany and risked all in a leaky ship to find freedom and found true religion in the newly formed *Deutsche evangelische Synode von Missouri, Ohio und anderen Staaten* (German Evangelical Synod of Missouri, Ohio and Other States). It will be a familiar place, not only because of the continuity with the old world but especially because it will be filled with the peace and presence of God. Best of all, we will hear that voice we know so well, the voice of the Good Shepherd who retains His wounds, calling us by name, gathering us in one holy communion, our hard pilgrimage finished at last, calling us to lie down beside the still waters.

The new heaven and earth will be unlike the first world and the present world in ways we have not experienced, as it is written: "What no eye has seen, nor ear heard, nor the heart of man imagined, what God has prepared for those who love Him" (1 Corinthians 2:9). There will be no marriage, for the need for reproduction will have ended; the full number of the elect will be there. We will know Jesus immediately and not through means. We will hear Him walking in the garden in the cool of the day, singing as He goes. We will see Him as He is, the evidence of things hoped for. The invisible will be visible: angels and archangels and cherubim and seraphim, circling around the throne of God our Father, higher and higher, like eagles, uttering clear, sharp cries of praise and thanksgiving without end.

Today we are declared righteous in God's sight by grace through faith in Christ. On that day, when we enter into the kingdom that has been prepared for us since the beginning of the world, we will be made holy: less than God in strength and knowledge but made equal to Him in holiness and eternity. All this is by the power of the resurrection. Our condition will then be *non posse peccare*. Forever. St. John speaks of the new heaven and the new earth, of the new Jerusalem, of how the dwelling place of God is with men, of how He will wipe away every tear from our eyes, of how death will be no more. Then "He who was seated on the throne said, 'Behold, I am making all things new'" (Revelation 21:5).

Endnotes

1 SC I (*LSCE*, 16).

2 Private conversation with Dr. David Menton, 2008.

3 See also Martin Luther's fine description in his *Lectures on Genesis* of what the "image of God" may have looked like for Adam before the fall into sin (AE 1:62):

> Therefore the image of God, according to which Adam was created, was something far more distinguished and excellent, since obviously no leprosy of sin adhered either to his reason or to his will. Both his inner and his outer sensations were all of the purest kind. His intellect was the clearest, his memory was the best, and his will was the most straightforward—all in the most beautiful tranquillity of mind, without any fear of death and without any anxiety. To these inner qualities came also those most beautiful and superb qualities of body and of all the limbs, qualities in which he surpassed all the remaining living creatures. I am fully convinced that before Adam's sin his eyes were so sharp and clear that they surpassed those of the lynx and eagle. He was stronger than the lions and the bears, whose strength is very great; and he handled them the way we handle puppies. Both the loveliness and the quality of the fruits he used as food were also far superior to what they are now.

4 Frederic W. Baue, *Creation: A Literary, Apologetic and Doctrinal Approach* (Naperville, IL: Blue Pomegranate Press, 2009).

5 See Louis A. Brighton, *Revelation*, Concordia Commentary (St. Louis: Concordia Publishing House, 1999), 352–53 (emphasis original):

> Many commentators today identify the beast of Rev 13:1–2 with the Roman Empire. In John's day, and long after, the beast of 13:1–2 did indeed represent Rome. After the fall of the Roman Empire in the fifth century, Rome continued to serve as the type and model of such tyrannical powers that would arise in the future. In light of this history, the interpretation includes Rome but also must be broadened: *the beast represents and symbolizes every human authority and everything of the human nature that the dragon can corrupt and control and use in his warfare against the woman (the church) and her seed (individual Christians)*: political, governmental, social, economic, philosophical, and educational systems, as well as individuals. No one entity or person at a given time in history will exhaust what the beast signifies.

CHRIST'S RESURRECTION IS JUSTIFICATION

Matthew C. Harrison

CHRIST'S resurrection is at the very heart of the "faith that was once for all delivered to the saints" (Jude 3) precisely because it is the justification of sinners before God. He "was delivered up for our trespasses and raised for our justification" (Romans 4:25).

Apostolic credentials to fill Judas's spot required one who "accompanied us during all the time that the Lord Jesus went in and out among us, beginning from the baptism of John" (Acts 1:21–22). Judas's replacement had to fulfill the chief apostolic task in his "office" (*episkope*, Acts 1:20)—that is, to be eyewitness to the resurrection of Christ (Acts 1:22; 3:15). Witnesses testify to the facts. Multiple witnesses multiply the legal veracity and reliability (Matthew 18:16; 26:60; Luke 24:48). The apostles bore witness in proclamation (Acts 3:15), and that witness coincided with the testimony of the Spirit about Christ (Acts 5:32), the testimony of Jesus about Himself, the testimony of the Father about Jesus, and the testimony of the Holy Scriptures all pointing to Jesus (John 5:32–47). The evangelists Matthew, Mark, Luke, and John (Matthew and John also being apostles) wrote their witness as a powerful eternal testimony for all of us who "have not seen and yet have believed" (John 20:29).

The eyewitness to Jesus' life, death, and resurrection burst forth into proclamation, fellowship, and joy for the apostle whom Jesus loved:

> That which was from the beginning, which we have heard, which we have seen with our eyes, which we looked upon and have touched with our hands, concerning the word of life—the life was made manifest, and we have seen it, and testify to it and proclaim to you the eternal life,

> which was with the Father and was made manifest to us—that which we have seen and heard we proclaim also to you, so that you too may have fellowship with us; and indeed our fellowship is with the Father and with His Son Jesus Christ. And we are writing these things so that our joy may be complete. (1 John 1:1–4)

> These [things] are written so that you may believe that Jesus is the Christ, the Son of God, and that by believing you may have life in His name. (John 20:31)

St. Paul asserts that to reject Jesus' teaching that the dead shall rise on the Last Day (John 11:25–26) is to reject Christ's own resurrection. The Corinthians had the temerity to deny "the resurrection of the body" but thought they would confess Christ's resurrection in some "spiritual" way just the same. So Paul argues for Christ's resurrection backward from the general resurrection: "For if the dead are not raised, not even Christ has been raised. And if Christ has not been raised, your faith is futile and you are still in your sins" (1 Corinthians 15:16–17). The bodily resurrection of Christ is the decisive event in history regarding sin and the eternal fate of sinners. Apostolic witnesses testify to its veracity and theological centrality.

What makes the accounts of Christ's resurrection credible? The fact that the texts of the New Testament are Christ's own word, divinely inspired, word-for-sacred-word, and thus powerful for creating belief in Christ ("living and active, sharper than any two-edged sword, piercing," Hebrews 4:12), and Jesus Himself promised the apostles the aid of the Holy Spirit in recounting salvific events (John 14:26). Three things are particularly compelling.

First, the Gospels are delightfully unified in the facts of Jesus' life, words, death, and resurrection, while at the same time marvelously and obviously written by different individuals. In some details they are aware of one another's texts, but they also include unique differences in theological emphases directed to varying audiences. Also, the precise order and emphases of parallel texts, together with discrete texts and accounts, is wondrously unique in the Gospels, bearing witness to complete uncontrived authenticity. The details of the resurrection appearances of Christ are unique to each Gospel writer, each with varying circumstances and details (sometimes defying harmonization), just what one would expect of real accounts.

Second, while those outside the early Christian community denied the resurrection from the beginning (Matthew 27:64), history records not a single example of a person who later came forward and asserted: "I was there. It did not happen" or even "I knew so-and-so who was there with

Jesus. He told me these things did not take place." An argument from silence, to be sure, but the silence is deafening!

Third, the historical evidence is completely unified in asserting the suffering and martyrdom of the apostles. This is borne witness to by Jesus (John 15:18), the earliest post-resurrection experience of the apostles (Acts 5:41), along with very strong early literary traditions. Also, in the past seventy-five years, there have been significant archeological finds for the martyrdoms of Peter and Paul. Other early traditions, such as St. Thomas's martyrdom in India, are very strong. Which leads me to this point: Why in the world would these dozen men burst upon the world with the message of the free forgiveness of sins and the promise of resurrection and eternal life because of the life, death, and resurrection of Jesus if it were not true? Sure, if it were the phantasmic vision of one person (such as Joseph Smith or Muhammad) or even of a few people, the matter would be much more problematic.

Paul's sober prose telling us of five hundred witnesses to the resurrection along with others, including himself, is forever compelling. It is even more compelling apologetically in light of the discovery in 2009 of the remains in the tomb of St. Paul, at the Basilica of St. Paul Outside the Walls in Rome, including Jewish clothing, of a first- or second-century man.[1]

> For I delivered to you as of first importance what I also received: that Christ died for our sins in accordance with the Scriptures, that He was buried, that He was raised on the third day in accordance with the Scriptures, and that He appeared to Cephas, then to the twelve. Then He appeared to more than five hundred brothers at one time, most of whom are still alive, though some have fallen asleep. Then He appeared to James, then to all the apostles. Last of all, as to one untimely born, He appeared also to me. For I am the least of the apostles, unworthy to be called an apostle, because I persecuted the church of God. But by the grace of God I am what I am, and His grace toward me was not in vain. On the contrary, I worked harder than any of them, though it was not I, but the grace of God that is with me. Whether then it was I or they, so we preach and so you believed. (1 Corinthians 15:3–11)

"Therefore, as one trespass led to condemnation for all men, so one act of righteousness leads to justification and life for all men" (Romans 5:18). The resurrection is justification. Christ "was delivered up for our trespasses and raised for our justification" (Romans 4:25). The resurrection is the justification of sinners.

If, as our great seventeenth-century Lutheran fathers put it, the resurrection is the grand absolution of the world in Christ, then it is also true that the resurrection makes no sense whatsoever without the doctrine of sin. If sin is no real damning problem, then consequent human foolishness mythologizes the resurrection of the Christ, and it floats off into "rejuvenation," "eternal optimism," or disembodied eternities in Platonic or Hindu realms of "spirit," waiting to "come back" in another form, all with a smiling Jesus who would not let Himself within a mile of a preached "Christ, the crucified one" (see 1 Corinthians 1:23). "Has not God made foolish the wisdom of the world?" (1 Corinthians 1:20).

Luther confesses for all true Lutherans and Christians that sin is more horrible than anyone can imagine. In fact, what the Bible tells us about it is so beyond the pale of reason that it must be believed. "The wages of sin is death" (Romans 6:23), temporal and eternal. The Lord told Adam in the garden: "But of the tree of the knowledge of good and evil you shall not eat, for in the day that you eat of it you shall surely die" (Genesis 2:17). The incessant drumbeat of death began.

The Bible teaches over and again that man is born blind, dead, and an enemy of God (see FC SD II), and humans invariably deny this stark truth, claiming some power or free will or even denying God altogether to claw back some illusion of autonomy.

> And you were dead in the trespasses and sins in which you once walked, following the course of this world, following the prince of the power of the air, the spirit that is now at work in the sons of disobedience—among whom we all once lived in the passions of our flesh, carrying out the desires of the body and the mind, and were by nature children of wrath, like the rest of mankind. (Ephesians 2:1–3)

To make light of sin is to make light of Christ. "The Son of Man came not to be served but to serve, and give His life as a ransom for many" (Mark 10:45). "For God so loved the world, that He gave His only Son" (John 3:16). The ransom was in the blood. "For the life of the flesh is in the blood, and I have given it for you on the altar to make atonement for your souls, for it is the blood that makes atonement by the life" (Leviticus 17:11). The blood of the Passover lamb marked the door of the faithful in Egypt. "They shall take some of the blood and put it on the two doorposts and the lintel of the houses in which they eat it" (Exodus 12:7). Luther's Easter hymn confesses Christ, whom St. Paul calls "our Passover lamb" who "has been sacrificed" (1 Corinthians 5:7):

> Here our true Paschal Lamb we see,
> Whom God so freely gave us;
> He died on the accursèd tree—
> So strong His love—to save us.

See, His blood now marks our door;
Faith points to it; death passes o'er,
And Satan cannot harm us.
Alleluia! (*LSB* 458:5)

The last and greatest prophet pointed to Christ: "Behold, the Lamb of God, who takes away the sin of the world!" (John 1:29). He is the eternal Son of God, God the Son (John 1:1). God the Son took on our flesh and blood (John 1:14). He fulfilled all the righteous requirements of the Law (Matthew 5:17; Galatians 4:4). He was conceived, was born, lived, suffered, died, and rose again—all without sin—for us (Hebrews 4:15; Romans 5:8; 8:32; Galatians 3:13; Ephesians 5:2; 1 Thessalonians 5:10; Titus 2:14; Hebrews 10:20). By the shedding of His precious and divine blood, He atoned for the sins of the world: "The blood of Jesus His Son cleanses us from all sin" (1 John 1:7). It was a blood ransom for a blood atonement for a blood redemption. Luther noted that if it were a mere man in the scales over against our sins, we would be lost. But the God-man and His divine blood outweigh the sins of the world.

No matter how offensive the divine remedy for sin, the remedy remains divine. The tax collector stands far off and prays: "God, be merciful to me, a sinner!" (Luke 18:13) The word translated "be merciful" (*hilaskomai*) means "to be favorably disposed," "conciliated," "propitiated." To "propitiate" is to regain favor by some act. In the New Testament, that act is Christ's to "make propitiation for the sins of the people" (Hebrews 2:17). The *hilasterion* is the very instrument by which God is appeased. The Lord Himself "set forth Christ as a *hilasterion*," as the means of atonement, expiation, removal of all the impediments to a gracious relationship with God Himself (Romans 3:25). The result is an objective justification of all people. St. Paul also says, "In Christ God was reconciling the world to Himself, not counting their trespasses against them" (2 Corinthians 5:19). So Paul can assert that "we regard no one according to the flesh" (2 Corinthians 5:16). There is no one whose sin is not paid for and covered. There is even a general justification of all. Jesus "was delivered up for our trespasses and raised for our justification" (Romans 4:25).

In 1 Timothy 3:14–16, Paul gives us one of the most compelling texts asserting the objective justification of sinners in Christ:

> I hope to come to you soon, but I am writing these things to you so that, if I delay, you may know how one ought to behave in the household of God, which is the church of the living God, a pillar and buttress of the truth. Great indeed, we confess, is the mystery of godliness:

> He was manifested in the flesh,
> vindicated by the Spirit,
> seen by angels,
> proclaimed among the nations,
> believed on in the world,
> taken up in glory.

Paul is asserting God "was manifested in the flesh." Indeed, "for our sake He made Him to be sin who knew no sin, so that in Him we might become the righteousness of God" (2 Corinthians 5:21). In Christ the sins of the world were damned. Christ "was manifested in the flesh" precisely for this purpose. The ESV then says "vindicated by the Spirit" (1 Timothy 3:16). "Vindicate" might give one the impression that this was Christ's personal vindication in the face of the false charges against His person (blasphemy, sedition). But this is not the meaning. "Vindicated" is the rendering of the original Greek word that means "justified." Christ was Himself "justified," declared "not guilty." Not guilty of what? The sins of the world. All those sins were damned in His person in death, absolved in His person by His resurrection, a transaction here specifically attributed to the Holy Spirit.

The deed is done, the gift accomplished. The most important things in the Christian faith were accomplished half a world away, some two thousand years ago. The objective acquired gifts of redemption are apprehended solely by faith in Christ and His blessed Gospel:

> For all have sinned and fall short of the glory of God, and [all!] are justified by His grace as a gift, through the redemption that is in Christ Jesus, whom God put forward as a propitiation [*hilasterion*, which means "rendering favorable"] by His blood, to be received by faith. (Romans 3:23–25)

In fact, just as Abraham's faith was "counted to him as righteousness," Paul continues, justification, or the declaration of righteousness, "will be counted to us who believe in Him who raised from the dead Jesus our Lord, who was delivered up for our trespasses and raised for our justification" (Romans 4:22, 24–25).

The resurrection is the justification of Christ, and it becomes my own by the Word proclaimed. "If you confess with your mouth that Jesus is Lord and believe in your heart that God raised Him from the dead, you will be saved. For with the heart one believes and is justified, and with the mouth one confesses and is saved" (Romans 10:9–10). Paul immediately proceeds to assert this message is preached into hearts. The resurrection is preached. When hearts believe the preaching of the resurrection, one "believes and is justified," that is, the objective reality is made one's own with all its benefits.

The ransom price is paid. No one will spend eternity in hell because the price of his or her redemption has not been paid in full nor because there has been no exoneration from sin. Hell is the consequence of seeking divine favor outside of Christ's justification. "No one comes to the Father except through Me" (John 14:6). Universalism is not the teaching of Jesus (see Matthew 25).

In Titus, Paul tells us that in addition to proclamation, Baptism delivers the objective realities of justification for the individual. Baptism is justification as it creates and is received by faith:

> But when the goodness and loving kindness of God our Savior appeared, He saved us, not because of works done by us in righteousness, but according to His own mercy, by the washing of regeneration and renewal of the Holy Spirit, whom He poured out on us richly through Jesus Christ our Savior, so that being justified by His grace we might become heirs according to the hope of eternal life. (Titus 3:4–7)

The justification of the sinner acquired by Christ is applied personally by the forgiveness delivered in absolution: "If you forgive the sins of any, they are forgiven them" (John 20:23), and received only by faith. Absolution is justification.

The justification of the sinner acquired by Christ is delivered by Christ's very body and blood in the Sacrament "given and shed for you for the forgiveness of sins." "For where there is forgiveness of sins, there is also life and salvation,"[2] that is, justification and resurrection! "Whoever feeds on My flesh and drinks My blood has eternal life, and I will raise him up on the last day. For My flesh is true food, and My blood is true drink" (John 6:54–55). The Lord's Supper is justification.

Christ's resurrection is nothing less than the justification of sinners, all sinners. Witnesses to the resurrection are compelling, be they apostles, evangelists, or, in a secondary sense, early traditions about the apostles and even archaeology. If Christ's resurrection did not happen, why would the apostles and their followers explode upon the world and be willing to die bearing witness to the resurrection? The resurrection is rendered unintelligible and unbiblical without a strong doctrine of sin and its horrid consequences. The resurrection of Christ is, first of all, *His* justification from the sins of the world! The justification brought by the resurrection is delivered by the proclamation of Christ's death and resurrection, by Baptism, by absolution, and by the Lord's Supper. The benefits of the death and resurrection of Christ are obtained solely by the repentant sinner who believes them.[3]

Endnotes

1 Pope Benedict XVI authorized the investigation of the tomb of St. Paul in 2009. Of the Vatican excavation of the tomb of St. Peter several decades earlier, Hermann Sasse wrote: "It cannot be proved, but it is very likely that they are authentic" ("Peter and Paul: Observations on the Origin of the Roman Primacy," *Reformed Theological Review* 24, no. 1 [1965]; repr., in *The Journal Articles of Hermann Sasse*, ed. Matthew C. Harrison, Bror Erickson, and Joel A. Brondos [Irvine: New Reformation Publications, 2016], 207 n. 8).

2 SC VI (*LSCE*, 29).

3 For one of the best presentations on the doctrine of justification, see Eduard Preuss, *The Justification of the Sinner before God: Explained from the Holy Scriptures* (Fort Wayne, IN: Lutheran Legacy, 2011). See also C. F. W. Walther, "The Reconciliation and Redemption of the Human Race," in *All Glory to God*, Walther's Works (St. Louis: Concordia Publishing House, 2016), 65–78.

THE GOD WHO SHOWS UP

John P. Lukomski

TO really appreciate the first Easter, we do well to remember that nobody thought Jesus was going to show up. Our Easter refrain may be "Christ is risen! He is risen indeed. Alleluia!" but their response was "He is risen. NOT!" We see this dramatically at the conclusion of Mark's Gospel, where the women "fled from the tomb, for trembling and astonishment had seized them, and they said nothing to anyone, for they were afraid" (Mark 16:8). Mark heaps up the negative words—"trembling," "astonishment," "fear." The word translated "fled" is the Greek word meaning to "flee for your life." This is not women running with joy to tell everyone "He is risen," but women running away as fast as they can in ecstatic terror.

At this point, my wife, Lynn, asked me if by "ecstatic terror" I meant they were joyfully terrified. I replied no—I meant that they were crazy with fear. She said I'd better look up ecstatic in the dictionary. She was right, as usual. In English, "ecstatic" means overwhelming happiness or joyful excitement. I had used the word "ecstatic" because it is the word Mark used. The Greek meaning is more "to be out of your mind." Using English figures of speech, Mark 16:8 would read "they ran for their lives, trembling like a leaf . . . out of their minds with fear." The women did not expect Jesus to show up and reacted accordingly. Compare this with Matthew, who says the women went to the disciples with "fear and great joy" (Matthew 28:8). So maybe they were joyfully terrified. Personally, I think Matthew is describing the women's emotions by the time they arrived at the disciples. Mark tells us how the women felt at first. The joy came later, as you'll see later in this essay.

Perhaps the women's trembling, astonishment, and fear can help us understand why, in Luke's Gospel, the disciples dismiss their testimony. The disciples thought the account from the women was an "idle tale, and they did not believe them" (Luke 24:11). Certainly, if someone came to us in a state of emotional disarray, we might question their veracity. Still the women's heightened response to a simple cemetery visit might make one think something significant had happened. That thought does not cross the disciples' minds because they have the same bias as the women. Jesus is dead, story over. Neither men nor women expected Jesus to show up Easter morning.

Yet Jesus did show up. This is the important point about the first Easter. Many people think Jesus only shows up if we believe. They think and act as if it is our faith that makes Jesus appear. The clear teaching of Scripture is that Jesus shows up whether we have faith or not. In the stories we now consider, He shows up precisely because people do not have faith. Apart from faith, as we have seen above, there is skepticism and fear. That is why Jesus wants us to have faith. Faith is His gift. If He does not show up, there will be no faith.

Let's look at this from a different angle. In one way, Jesus does not have to show up, because He is already there. As the Son of God, He is always here, showering us with earthly blessing. He even does this "to all evil people."[1] However, He wants to give us a greater blessing, a spiritual blessing, called faith. Yes, Jesus wants us to know earthly blessings are from Him. But more than that, He wants us to know that He blesses us even in tribulation. He wants us to know that He blesses us even when we sin. Indeed, His greatest blessing is the forgiveness of sins. The earthly blessings come easy. Jesus just shows up and gives them, as He did throughout His ministry—healing the sick, calming storms, feeding thousands. But for the spiritual blessing of faith, Jesus must show up in a different way. He must show up in a way that goes beyond what we can reason, see, or feel.

To understand this special way Jesus shows up to give us the special blessing of faith, consider two of the greatest doubters in the Easter story. Their stories are detailed in John 20. The first doubter is Mary Magdalene. While the rest of the women ran away, Mary remained. We can speculate as to why. Maybe the other women went to the tomb out of a sense of duty, to make sure things had been done correctly. After all, what would a rich man such as Joseph of Arimathea know about the critical details of preparing a body for burial? This was women's work. If you want a job done right, you know who to ask. Whatever the motives of the other women, it was a very personal task for Mary, one final visitation of the Lord she had loved. As John tells us, "Mary stood weeping outside the tomb" (John 20:11). Maybe it was this grief that kept her there at the tomb, overriding her fear.

Yet even with all her devotion to the Lord, she could not shake her unbelief. Despite all the things Mary saw, her doubt remained. She saw an empty tomb. She saw two angels who spoke to her. Still there was no faith. The stubbornness of her unbelief is shown in verse 14: "She turned around and saw Jesus standing, but she did not know that it was Jesus." She sees Jesus standing in front of her, but she still does not believe. Even after Jesus speaks to her, "Woman, why are you weeping?" (v. 15), she still does not believe. Supposing Him to be a cemetery worker, she asks Him if He moved the body. Her unbelief ends only when Jesus says to her, "Mary." Then the spiritual blessing of faith comes upon Mary as she exclaims, "Teacher!" and holds on to Jesus for dear life (John 20:16).

John is illustrating that faith does not come from what we see or what we feel. Jesus showing up physically does not give Mary faith. Rather, Jesus' word gives faith. It is a personal word to Mary. It is a personal word to us. In the Lord's Supper Jesus says, "My body, which is given for you" and "My blood, which is shed for you." In the Small Catechism, Luther says it is the words "for you" that bring about a truly believing heart.[2] This is how Jesus shows up for us—in His Word.

To further this point, John describes the disciples in an Upper Room on Easter evening. Again, no one is expecting Jesus to show up. As with the women, the controlling emotion is fear. "On the evening of that day, the first day of the week, the doors being locked where the disciples were for fear of the Jews" (John 20:19). However, as with Mary, despite their fear and doubt, Jesus still shows up. He speaks a personal word, "Peace be with you." Unlike the women, the men do not run away in fear but rather "were glad when they saw the Lord" (John 20:20).

Before my male readers point out how cool, calm, and collected the men's reactions were to Jesus' surprise appearance, consider this. In contrast to His appearance to the women, Jesus' showing up was not a total surprise to the men. Two of their number had testified that they had seen Jesus on the road to Emmaus. They also had the witness of the women. If anything, the men had egg on their face for their earlier comment about the women's "idle tale." I know my wife would not let me forget a remark like that, and I doubt those women did either. Furthermore, there is some question of just how calm and collected the men were. After all, Jesus had to say to them a second time, "Peace be with you" (John 20:21).

Whatever the emotional state of the disciples, the scene is set for the second greatest doubter of Easter—Thomas. Faith should have been easier for Thomas than for Mary. True, he did not see the empty tomb. But an open tomb is ambiguous evidence at best. As Mary (and John and Peter) understood, someone simply could have moved the body. True, Thomas didn't see any angels, but angels are overrated. Many think all they need for faith is a heavenly vision. But according to Scripture, angels are received with fear and skepticism. This is the response of Zechariah (Luke 1:12) and the shepherds (Luke 2:9). Even the mother of our Lord says to the angel Gabriel: "How will this be?" (Luke 1:34). Such suspicion of heavenly signs is warranted because, as Paul says, "even Satan disguises himself as an angel of light" (2 Corinthians 11:14). However, what Thomas had was greater than empty tombs or angels. He had the testimony of ten eyewitnesses. Scripture itself only requires two or three witnesses to establish the truth of a matter. Yet Thomas remains the strongest of unbelievers, announcing: "Unless I see in His hands the mark of the nails, and place my finger into the mark of the nails, and place my hand into His side, I will never believe" (John 20:25).

Certainly such a powerful statement of unbelief—"I will never believe"—should discourage Jesus from showing up: "Who are you, Thomas, to doubt Me? Especially when I have sent you so many witnesses." At least that is how I would have felt, but not Jesus. If you tell Jesus you will not believe, He is all the more determined that you will believe.

A week later the disciples were in the Upper Room again, and Thomas was with them. Note again that "the doors were locked" (John 20:26). Whatever faith the disciples had a week earlier had again been replaced by fear. That is the problem with faith based on sight. It lasts only as long as you can see the thing in which you hope. Despite Thomas's doubt or the doubt of the other disciples, Jesus showed up once again. Not only did He show up, but He also spoke that personal word of comfort again: " 'Peace be with you.' Then He said to Thomas, 'Put your finger here, and see My hands; and put out your hand, and place it in My side' " (John 20:26–27). These are the very words spoken by Thomas earlier. Although Thomas and the disciples were unaware of it, Jesus had been with them all along. He heard every word of their conversation with Thomas. Faith understands that Jesus is always with us in peace, whether we see Him or not.

As I mentioned, one might think that Thomas's hard-hearted statement "I will never believe" might have put Jesus off. After all, Jesus had given Thomas ten solid witnesses. Shouldn't that be enough? Understand that Jesus is resolute that Thomas (as well as you and I) believe. Thus Jesus acquiesced to Thomas's request and showed him His hands and feet. Jesus declared, "Do not disbelieve but believe" (John 20:27). He then gave Thomas (and us) a warning. Thomas's desire to see and touch will not give him the faith that he needs. It might make him glad for the moment, but it will not sustain him for the trials that lie ahead. So Jesus continued: "Have you believed because you have seen Me? Blessed are those who have not seen and yet have believed" (John 20:29).

This verse is precisely the personal "for us" words of Jesus mentioned earlier. We are the ones Jesus is talking about. We are the blessed ones. We have not seen and yet have believed. We have seen neither empty tomb nor angels nor the bodily hands and feet of Jesus. Yet we believe. How is that possible? How has Jesus shown up so that we have this blessed faith?

John explains the special way Jesus shows up for us in the next verses of his Gospel: "Now Jesus did many other signs in the presence of the disciples, which are not written in this book; but these are written so that you may believe that Jesus is the Christ, the Son of God, and that by believing you may have life in His name" (John 20:30–31). The things that create a true faith are the things that "are written" in Holy Scripture. As we have seen in the case of Mary and Thomas, even the visible presence of Jesus is not enough to give us the faith we need. Real faith is ours only when Jesus shows up in His Word. It is not the appearance of Jesus but the Word of Jesus that creates faith. These are not empty words but living words that speak personally to us. Words that tell us that we are forgiven. Words that say, "Peace be *with you*." Words that tell us *we* have life in His name.

For the apostle John, this is an important issue. Jesus has ascended into heaven. The other disciples have been martyred. John is the last man standing. Soon the final eyewitness to the resurrection of Jesus will be gone. The last one who "saw" the signs that Jesus did will depart. Does this mark the end of the church? Will faith cease with the death of the last witness? No, because faith does not depend on sight but on the words that Jesus has spoken. The "Scriptures" are the words that Jesus' Spirit inspired His chosen apostles to write down—words that were spoken to them, to us, and to all, until the end of time. Words spoken to all those, like us, who have not seen and yet have believed. Blessed faith is not our work but the gift given us by Jesus' word.

John confesses that even he did not understand faith at first. He, too, thought one had to see and feel things to truly believe. In the beginning of chapter 20, John talks about going with Peter to the tomb. They saw it was obvious that no one had moved the body. All the grave linens were neatly folded and carefully placed. If someone had moved the body, they would not take the time to unwrap it so neatly. Witnessing the pristine condition of the tomb, John says of himself that he "saw and believed" (John 20:8). But John then makes this confession: "as yet they did not understand the Scripture, that He must rise from the dead" (John 20:9). John did not need to see an empty tomb, angels, or even the resurrected Jesus to believe. The Scriptures were enough. Even for the great apostle, faith was not a matter of what he had seen but rather a matter of the things written in the Bible. Even for John, his faith was not primarily about what he had seen but the words of Jesus that he had heard.

Faith is not a thing we do. It is not something within us that brings Jesus into our presence. Faith is not a thing that makes Jesus show up in our lives. In a very real sense Jesus is always present in our lives. He promises: "Behold, I am with you always, to the end of the age" (Matthew 28:20). He can show up in a variety of ways. We see Him in the good things in our lives. Like the Wise Men, we see the star and rejoice (Matthew 2:10). We see Him in our loving friends and family. The word *angel* means "messenger." These people are our "angels" sent from Jesus. In all these things Jesus comes to us, even as He came to Mary, Thomas, and the rest, because it is His desire that we "do not disbelieve, but believe." But good times and good friends are not always present in our lives, even as Jesus was not always physically present for the disciples. True, lasting, permanent faith cannot rest on what we see, experience, or feel. That faith can come only from the Scriptures. These Scriptures tell us that in our Baptism we are saved (1 Peter 3:21), that in the Lord's Supper our sins are forgiven (Matthew 26:28), and that "neither death nor life, nor angels nor rulers, nor things present nor things to come, nor powers, nor height nor depth, nor anything else in all creation, will be able to separate us from the love of God in Christ Jesus our Lord" (Romans 8:38–39). This is the way Jesus shows up to give us blessed faith. "These [things] are written so that you may believe" (John 20:31).

Epilogue

It puzzled me that the women who fled the tomb and "said nothing to anyone, for they were afraid" (Mark 16:8) are later able to tell "all these things to the eleven and to all the rest" (Luke 24:9). What happened to their debilitating panic? Matthew tells us that Jesus showed up for the women just as He had shown up for Mary and Thomas. As they ran from the tomb, "behold, Jesus met them and said, 'Greetings!' And they came up and took hold of His feet and worshiped Him. Then Jesus said to them, 'Do not be afraid; go and tell My brothers to go to Galilee, and there they will see Me' " (Matthew 28:9–10). It is these personal words of Jesus that replace their fear with faith. Consider the striking phrase in Luke's resurrection account:

"They remembered *His words,* and returning from the tomb they told all these things to the eleven and to all the rest" (Luke 24:8–9, emphasis added). It is not so much the appearance of Jesus but the words of Jesus that gave them faith. They spoke these words to others that they might have faith. It is these same words that give us faith. The Jesus we need is the Jesus who "shows up" in His Word of Good News.

Endnotes

1 SC III (*LSCE*, 21).

2 See SC VI (*LSCE*, 29): "Who receives this sacrament worthily? Fasting and bodily preparation are certainly fine outward training. But that person is truly worthy and well prepared who has faith in these words: 'Given and shed for you for the forgiveness of sins.' But anyone who does not believe these words or doubts them is unworthy and unprepared, for the words 'for you' require all hearts to believe."

RESURRECTION AND BAPTISM IN ROMANS

Jacob T. Mueller

EVERY time someone is baptized in our congregation, I marvel at the simplicity of it all. Of course, there are the prayers, blessings, Scripture passages, and a confession of faith, but the part that really matters is very simple. Call the person by name, say the words Jesus commanded—"I baptize you in the name of the Father and of the Son and of the Holy Spirit" (see Matthew 28:19)—and pour water over their head as you say it. Thankfully, even if I suddenly forget the name, our church displays a banner with the person's name less than three feet from my eyeballs.

God could have made this much more complicated—just look at the sacrifices and rites in Leviticus. There is great complexity and sometimes more information than a sensitive stomach can handle. I would have been worried about messing up the sacrifices and offending the Lord, if I had been an Old Testament priest!

This simple act of Baptism makes Easter more than just an event that happened once a long time ago. Jesus lives for you and meets you in the water. That changes your reality right now and gives you hope for eternity. Through this washing, God gives you a direct connection with Jesus' resurrection.

Do not let the simplicity of Baptism fool you. It does not require much from the pastor because it is the Lord Himself who is doing the baptizing. He is the one giving the gifts, and those gifts are incredible. The simplicity of Baptism is not a comfort for pastors only but for everyone who is baptized. In this essay, we will explore how this simple washing connects us with Jesus' resurrection using examples from Paul's letter to the Romans.

1. Baptism and Resurrection

Paul's letter to the church in Rome explains what God has done for us in Jesus by raising Him from the dead. While the primary focus of Romans is God's action, that action is for us (Romans 8:31). We can be certain that God acts for us because in the waters of Baptism we were united with Jesus in His death and resurrection.

Peter's Pentecost sermon about Jesus' resurrection was the first time that people from Rome heard this good news. Those from Rome included both Jews and converts to Judaism (Acts 2:10–11), and some of them must have been included in the three thousand people who were baptized that day (Acts 2:41). When Paul wrote his letter to the church at Rome, he wrote to people already convinced that God raised Jesus from the dead. He did not have to prove to them that Jesus had risen as he did with the Corinthians (see 1 Corinthians 15). The section on Baptism opens with the question "Do you not know?" (Romans 6:3), implying that the Romans already understood the connection between Baptism and Jesus' resurrection (see Romans 15:14–15).

These two themes from the day of Pentecost—Jesus' resurrection and the life of a baptized Christian—are key themes in Paul's letter to Rome. Romans 6:1–11 presents one of the most extensive teachings on Baptism in the New Testament. Here Paul clearly connects our Baptism with Jesus' resurrection:

> What shall we say then? Are we to continue in sin that grace may abound? By no means! How can we who died to sin still live in it? Do you not know that all of us who have been baptized into Christ Jesus were baptized into His death? We were buried therefore with Him by baptism into death, in order that, just as Christ was raised from the dead by the glory of the Father, we too might walk in newness of life.
>
> For if we have been united with Him in a death like His, we shall certainly be united with Him in a resurrection like His. We know that our old self was crucified with Him in order that the body of sin might be brought to nothing, so that we would no longer be enslaved to sin. For one who has died has been set free from sin. Now if we have died with Christ, we believe that we will also live with Him. We know that Christ, being raised from the dead, will never die again; death no longer has dominion over Him. For the death He died He died to sin, once for all, but the life He lives He lives to God. So you also must consider yourselves dead to sin and alive to God in Christ Jesus. (Romans 6:1–11)

While this is the only place in Romans that Paul specifically addresses Baptism, he refers to Jesus' resurrection throughout the epistle. Since Paul made the connection between Jesus' resurrection and our Baptism in Romans 6:1–11, the other references to Easter also have something to say about our lives as baptized believers in Christ.

2. Baptism and Justification

Baptism changes our lives right now. First and foremost, Baptism brings us Christ and His forgiveness for our sins (Acts 2:38). We become part of His Body (1 Corinthians 12:13; Ephesians 4:4–5) and put on Christ (Galatians 3:27), and in Christ God declares us not guilty because Jesus rose from the dead (Romans 8:1). Our lives are changed because we are not left wondering what God thinks of us. His love and forgiveness are certain.

Some may object that since we are saved by faith (Romans 3–4; Ephesians 2:8), Baptism should not be part of the discussion of salvation, or that babies cannot confess their faith and therefore should not be baptized. But God's Word makes crystal clear the connection between Baptism, the Holy Spirit, and the way we receive faith. The Holy Spirit is active every time someone is baptized (Mark 1:8; Acts 2:38; Titus 3:5) and gives the faith that trusts in Jesus' resurrection that justifies and saves (John 15:26; 16:14; Romans 8:10; 10:9; 1 Corinthians 12:3; Ephesians 1:13). This is why Scripture says Baptism saves (Mark 16:16; John 3:3–7; 1 Peter 3:21). Baptism saves because Jesus saves. In Baptism, we are united with Christ, receive faith in Him through the Holy Spirit, and are completely forgiven. Since Baptism is God's work, He can do this to whomever He wants—no matter how young or old they are. God's Word makes it clear that He wants this to happen to everyone (Matthew 28:19–20; Acts 2:39).[1]

In Baptism, we share in Jesus' death because we need to die. There our old self, the body of sin, is nailed to the cross with Jesus and done away with completely (Romans 6:6). Martin Luther explains this in his 1520 book, *The Babylonian Captivity of the Church*:

> It is therefore indeed correct to say that baptism is a washing away of sins, but the expression is too mild and weak to bring out the full significance of baptism, which is rather a symbol of death and resurrection. . . .
>
> The sinner does not so much need to be washed as he needs to die, in order to be wholly renewed and made another creature, and to be conformed to the death and resurrection of Christ, with whom he dies and rises again through baptism. (AE 36:68)

Since we are united with Jesus in Baptism, God now declares us "not guilty." We are justified. Even though we have sinned, God declares us righteous. Earlier, Paul connected Jesus' resurrection directly with our justification—one of the most important themes in Romans: "It [righteousness] will be counted to us who believe in Him who raised from the dead Jesus our Lord, who was delivered up for our trespasses and raised for our justification. Therefore, since we have been justified by faith, we have peace with God through our Lord Jesus Christ" (Romans 4:24–5:1).

Previously, when Paul described justification in Romans 3:21–26, he described God's action in a way that makes us think more of Good Friday than Easter. Jesus was "put forward as a propitiation by His blood" (Romans 3:25). God poured out His anger on Jesus as He shed His blood for us. But in Romans 4, Paul makes the clear connection between justification and Jesus' resurrection: both go together. As it is written in 1 Corinthians 15:17, "if Christ has not been raised, your faith is futile and you are still in your sins." Paul also clearly connects justification and Baptism in 1 Corinthians 6:11 and Titus 3:4–7.

Baptism changes our lives because God forgives our sins for Jesus' sake. Yes, our sins are very real and very many! But God declares us "not guilty" because we are in Christ, and we can be sure that we are in Christ because we have been baptized into His name (Matthew 28:19; Acts 2:38).

3. Baptism and Our New Life

What does this changed life look like right now? The immediate context of Romans 6:1–11 shows us how Baptism leads us to walk new lives. At the end of Romans 5, Paul explains how, as sin increased, God's grace increased even more. Adam's rebellion against God led to sin and death, which have spread to all people. Since that is true, God's free gift of righteousness has overflowed even more to cover sins (Romans 5:15–21)!

So if sin makes God's grace increase, then why not sin more? After all, who wouldn't want more grace, more love, and more forgiveness from God? Sinning more should yield more of those things. But Paul objects! "How can we who died to sin still live in it?" (Romans 6:2). We cannot! Our relationship to sin has changed. We were slaves to sin, but we died. "For one who has died has been set free from sin" (Romans 6:7). Yes, forgiveness is good, but avoiding sin is also good. Since we are dead to sin, we should want to serve God and others rather than ourselves.

Working for sin, we deserve death. Instead of getting what we deserve, God gives us what Jesus' resurrection brings: "For the wages of sin is death, but the free gift of God is eternal life in Christ Jesus our Lord" (Romans 6:23). We will struggle with sin for the rest of our lives

(Romans 7:13–25), but we know God's final verdict for us: "There is therefore now no condemnation for those who are in Christ Jesus" (Romans 8:1). How do we know that we are "in Christ Jesus"? We need only turn back two chapters to read: "All of us who have been baptized into Christ Jesus were baptized into His death" (Romans 6:3); "our old self was crucified with Him" (Romans 6:6); and "if we have died with Christ, we believe that we will also live with Him" (Romans 6:8).

In view of this mercy, God helps us live a new life. In the Small Catechism, Luther uses Romans 6:4 to answer the question

> *What does such baptizing with water signify?*
>
> It indicates that the Old Adam in us should by daily contrition and repentance be drowned and die with all sins and evil desires, and that a new man should daily emerge and arise to live before God in righteousness and purity forever.[2]

Through our Baptism into Jesus' resurrection, God helps us "to walk in newness of life" (Romans 6:4). Instead of doing what our flesh wants to do, we do the good things that the Holy Spirit helps us do (Romans 8:5–7). Instead of being conformed to the way the world thinks, God transforms the way our minds work so we want to do the good and gracious will of God (Romans 12:2).

4. Jesus' Resurrection Proves God Will Keep His Promises

Connecting our Baptism to Jesus' resurrection gives us confidence in God's promises, especially when we face death. Paul begins Romans by reminding us how God's promises were kept when Jesus rose from the dead. The Gospel was "promised beforehand through His prophets in the holy Scriptures" (Romans 1:2) and made clear by Jesus' resurrection from the dead (Romans 1:1–4).

The Old Testament points clearly to Jesus' resurrection. In Psalm 16, David expresses his confidence to the Lord in the face of death: "For You will not abandon my soul to Sheol, or let Your holy one see corruption" (Psalm 16:10). Peter explains that David was talking about Jesus (Acts 2:25–31). David's body decayed, but Jesus' body did not. He is alive again!

Both Jesus (Matthew 21:33–42 || Mark 12:1–11 || Luke 20:9–18) and Peter (Acts 4:10–12; 1 Peter 2:7) use Psalm 118:22–23 to describe not only Jesus' death but also His resurrection. Jesus is "the stone that the builders rejected" and killed, but God raised Him from the dead and made Him "the cornerstone" (Psalm 118:22), and now "there is salvation in no one else" (Acts 4:12). Indeed, "this is the LORD's doing; it is marvelous in our eyes" (Psalm 118:23).

Other Old Testament passages promise Jesus' resurrection. Jonah's life previews Jesus' resurrection. His three days and nights in the fish (Jonah 1:17; 2:10) foreshadow God's greatest miracle of all time—Jesus' resurrection (Matthew 12:38–41). There are, of course, others in the Old Testament whose lives foreshadowed Jesus' resurrection. Isaac (Romans 4:17–19); Joseph (Genesis 50:20); Shadrach, Meshach, and Abednego (Daniel 3:19–28); and Daniel (Daniel 6:16–23) are just a few examples.

God promised to send Jesus and raise Him from the dead. What does that mean for our life in Christ? Here's the good news: we know God keeps His promises. When you were baptized, God made promises to you. He promised to forgive your sins and give you the Holy Spirit (Acts 2:38). The Holy Spirit promised to renew and regenerate you (Titus 3:5). God promised to save you (Mark 16:16; 1 Peter 3:21) and bring you into His kingdom (John 3:3–5).

If God made the promise to send Jesus and raise Him from the dead and kept that promise, then you can be sure that He will keep the promises of forgiveness, life, and salvation that He has made to you in your Baptism.

It happens to all of us on our worst days. The devil comes along and says, "Sure, it says 'for God so loved the world,' but how could He love you after what you've done?" In Baptism, God makes those promises of love, forgiveness, and everlasting life directly to you. You may doubt your own thoughts or feelings, but in Baptism God has done something for you—yes, you. You were called by name. The water touched your head. You can be certain of God's love for you in Baptism.

This is why some of the traditions that we use to help children (and the rest of us) remember our Baptism are very helpful. This begins with the ancient tradition of sponsors. Parents choose people who will remind their children: "Yep, you were baptized; I saw it happen!" Uncle Herb was, and Aunt Faith still is, one of my sponsors. Their encouragement throughout my life is a blessing to this day. In addition to sponsors, we now take pictures and perhaps even videos of Baptisms. Congregations give baptismal certificates, banners, and candles. Families are encouraged to mark baptismal birthdays. This is all to remind us of the sure and certain promises God has made in the waters of Baptism.

5. Constant Love from God

Again and again, Romans reminds us of God's constant love. For example, Romans 5:10 explains: "For if while we were enemies we were reconciled to God by the death of His Son, much more, now that we are reconciled, shall we be saved by His life." Imagine this: You have a neighbor whom you do not necessarily like, but this person undergoes surgery. So you bring a meal during the recovery because you know you should. But consider how much different your attitude would be if your best friend experienced the same thing and you brought your friend a meal to help during the recovery. You would do that with joy! That joy which you have in serving your best friend is the love that God showed when Jesus died for us, His enemies. But we are not God's enemies anymore, and Jesus is not dead anymore. Think of how much more love God will give us! Ambrosiaster, in his *Commentary on Paul's Epistles*, explains it this way: "So if he died for his enemies, just think what he will do for his friends!"[3]

Here are a few ways that love shows itself even now. We have direct access to God our Father and the Holy Spirit to help even when we can't come up with words for prayer (Romans 8:26–27). Our Baptism into Jesus' resurrection means that God is for us (Romans 8:31). If He did not spare His Son but gave Jesus up for us, "how will He not also with Him graciously give us all things?" (Romans 8:32). Since He has declared us "not guilty," there is no higher power that can bring any charge against us. We are connected to Jesus, who sits at God's right hand on our behalf (Romans 8:33–34).

6. Baptism and Our Resurrection

It is not as though God has promised something small either. No! His promises are more powerful than death itself. It is one thing to promise material blessings or victory in battle. Those things could seemingly happen on their own. But God promises to do something only He can do—give us eternal life. Since Jesus rose again from the dead, we can be certain that God will keep that promise to us as well. The Holy Spirit's work in us, which is promised in Baptism, means that the same thing will happen to us as happened to Jesus. Paul explains what the word of the Holy Spirit means in the face of death:

> Although the body is dead because of sin, the Spirit is life because of righteousness. If the Spirit of Him who raised Jesus from the dead dwells in you, He who raised Christ Jesus from the dead will also give life to your mortal bodies through His Spirit who dwells in you. (Romans 8:10–11)

The same Holy Spirit who descended on Jesus in the form of a dove at His Baptism (Matthew 3:16 || Mark 1:10 || Luke 3:22; John 1:32–33) lives in you now because of your Baptism (Acts 2:38). The Holy Spirit is the down payment of our eternal life (Ephesians 1:14). Jesus died and was buried, and we will die and be buried. But Jesus rose again, and we will too. This is the best news for someone who is dying, a family who is mourning, or friends who are gathered at a funeral. Jesus will keep this promise and one day raise our bodies just as He rose from the dead.

Nothing—not even death—can separate us from the love that God has for us in Jesus Christ (Romans 8:37–39). Death cannot rule over Jesus anymore (Romans 6:9). Because death does not rule over Jesus, it will not be our lord either. Since Jesus died and rose again, He will always be our Lord. While we live, we live for the Lord. When we die, our death is different because we still belong to Jesus. We are not lost, because He is still our Lord. Jesus died and rose again so that He will always be our Lord (Romans 14:8–9).

In Baptism, your whole life is wrapped up in Christ. Because He rose from the dead, your life goes beyond the grave. Jesus rose, and so will you. God works in such simple ways to give you the most comfort possible. He does not want to leave you doubting His love, so He makes it clear and certain in Baptism. Just as He raised Jesus from the dead, He has also brought you new life now and will give you life forever.

Endnotes

1 In my adult instruction classes for people who have not been baptized, I always remind them that if they are hit by a semi on the way home from class before they are baptized, they will still be saved since they already have faith in Jesus. Romans 10:9 says, "If you confess with your mouth that Jesus is Lord and believe in your heart that God raised Him from the dead, you will be saved." Jesus saves and God brings us that salvation through His Word as well as Baptism.

2 SC IV (*LSCE*, 24).

3 *ACCS* NT 6:131.

WITHOUT THE RESURRECTION OF JESUS THERE IS NO CHURCH, EVER!

John C. Wohlrabe Jr.

IT is interesting how an order of things can be intricately relational but may then go unnoticed or unrecognized. Take the three articles of the Apostles' Creed and Nicene Creed, for example. Here Christians throughout the ages and across the globe confess both the Holy Christian Church and the resurrection of the dead and the life everlasting. These actually go together. We could even say they are inseparable. One results from the other. Furthermore, our membership in the church and our resurrection on the Last Day unto life everlasting are direct results of Christ's resurrection, which is confessed in the Second Article of these creeds. Because of this order and relation, we can be so bold as to say that "without the resurrection of Jesus there is no church, ever!" Our membership in the Holy Christian Church and our resurrection unto eternal life on the Last Day rest on the factuality and meaning of Jesus Christ's rising from the grave that first Easter morn.

The apostle Paul discusses the reality of the resurrection of Jesus and what this means for Christians in the fifteenth chapter of his first letter to the church in Corinth. Here we read the following:

> Now I would remind you, brothers, of the gospel I preached to you, which you received, in which you stand, and by which you are being saved, if you hold fast to the word I preached to you—unless you believed in vain.
>
> For I delivered to you as of first importance what I also received: that Christ died for our sins in accordance with the Scriptures, that He was buried, that He was raised on the third day in accordance with the

> Scriptures, and that He appeared to Cephas, then to the twelve. Then He appeared to more than five hundred brothers at one time, most of whom are still alive, though some have fallen asleep. . . .
>
> Now if Christ is proclaimed as raised from the dead, how can some of you say that there is no resurrection of the dead? But if there is no resurrection of the dead, then not even Christ has been raised. And if Christ has not been raised, then our preaching is in vain and your faith is in vain. We are even found to be misrepresenting God, because we testified about God that He raised Christ, whom He did not raise if it is true that the dead are not raised. For if the dead are not raised, not even Christ has been raised. And if Christ has not been raised, your faith is futile and you are still in your sins. Then those also who have fallen asleep in Christ have perished. If in Christ we have hope in this life only, we are of all people most to be pitied.
>
> But in fact Christ has been raised from the dead, the firstfruits of those who have fallen asleep. (1 Corinthians 15:1–6, 12–20)

St. Paul articulates several very important truths concerning the resurrection of Jesus in this initial epistle to the Corinthian Church. First, the resurrection is an indisputable fact. It was witnessed not only by the apostles but also by more than five hundred others, most of whom were alive at the time that Paul was writing to the church in Corinth around AD 55. Now, if this were a fabrication, there would certainly be evidence of people coming forward to deny the assertion of Paul and the other apostles. This epistle was written just more than twenty years after Christ's resurrection. Think back twenty or so years to significant incidents in your own life, particularly significant occurrences that you shared and witnessed with others. Those memories remain and are often reminisced upon, discussed, mutually verified, and validated by those with whom you shared the event.

Second, the resurrection of Jesus was an essential part of the Gospel that Paul and the other apostles preached, which brings salvation to those who believe. Paul first points to Christ's death for our sins and His burial; but without our Lord's resurrection on the third day, the Gospel would be incomplete (see also 2 Timothy 2:8). To the Galatians (1:8), Paul would even state that anyone who preaches a different gospel is accursed.

Third, if Jesus did not rise from the dead, our faith in Him is futile. Then Jesus is not who He said He is, and then Jesus did not do what He said He would do (Matthew 16:20–21 || Mark 8:29–31 || Luke 9:21–22; John 10:30; 11:25–26; 14:6).

Fourth, and this is vital for our understanding of the nature of the church, without Jesus' resurrection, there is no forgiveness of sins. Paul makes that very clear in 1 Corinthians 15. But, in fact, Jesus rose from the grave to conquer sin, death, and the devil. The resurrection of Jesus Christ is so significant because it shows us that He truly is the Son of God (Romans 1:4). Furthermore, it means that all He taught is true (John 2:19; 8:28). It verifies that God the Father accepted Jesus' sacrifice for the reconciliation of the world (Romans 4:25; 5:10). Finally, it means that all believers in Christ will also rise to eternal life (John 11:25–26; 14:19; 1 Corinthians 15:20).

What connects the resurrection of the body and life everlasting to the "holy Christian Church, the communion of saints" in the Apostles' Creed is the "forgiveness of sins." What joins the resurrection of the dead and the life of the world to come to "the holy Christian and apostolic Church" in the Nicene Creed is "one Baptism for the remission of sins." In both cases, our resurrection to glory in the Third Article is connected to Christ's resurrection in the Second Article because it is made possible through the forgiveness of sins that comes to the Holy Christian Church by way of Christ's rising from the dead.

Beginning in the late eighteenth century and early nineteenth century, mainly through the teaching of Friedrich Schleiermacher, many viewed the church as predominately a social expression of people's religious feelings. But this is not what the church is all about. It is not a social organization based on people's feelings and their decision to join.

Martin Luther wrote in the explanation of the Third Article of the Apostles' Creed in the Small Catechism:

> I believe that I cannot by my own reason or strength believe in Jesus Christ, my Lord, or come to Him; but the Holy Spirit has called me by the Gospel, enlightened me with His gifts, sanctified and kept me in the true faith. In the same way He calls, gathers, enlightens, and sanctifies the whole Christian church on earth, and keeps it with Jesus Christ in the one true faith. In this Christian church He daily and richly forgives all my sins and the sins of all believers. On the Last Day He will raise me and all the dead, and give eternal life to me and all believers in Christ. This is most certainly true.[1]

According to Article VIII of the Augsburg Confession, "strictly speaking, the Church is the congregation of saints and true believers" (AC VIII 1). Martin Luther stated in the Smalcald Articles: "Thank God, [today] a seven-year-old child knows what the Church is, namely, the holy believers and lambs who hear the voice of their Shepherd [John 10:11–16]" (SA III XII 2, brackets original).

The existence of the church depends on the forgiveness of sins. And the forgiveness of sins depends on the life, death, and resurrection of Jesus

Christ, each point of which makes up the core of the Gospel message. People do not decide to associate with the church based on mutual religious feelings. Rather, the Holy Spirit calls believers to faith through the Gospel purely taught and proclaimed and the sacraments correctly administered. The Holy Christian Church is the gathering of true believers in the salvation that comes through Jesus' life, death, and resurrection for the forgiveness of sins. These are true believers across the world and across time.

In his work *The Church and the Office of the Ministry*, the theses of which were adopted by The Lutheran Church—Missouri Synod in 1851, C. F. W. Walther states in his first thesis:

> The Church [*Kirche*] in the proper sense [*eigentlichen Sinne*] of the word is the congregation [*Gemeinde*] of saints, that is, the entirety [*Gesamtheit*] of all those who, called out of the lost and condemned human race by the Holy Spirit through the Word, truly believe in Christ and by faith are sanctified and incorporated in Christ.[2]

Not only is it important to observe that this church consists only of those true believers called by God's Word and sanctified (made righteous through the forgiveness of sins) by faith in Jesus Christ, but this church is the "entirety" of those called from creation to Judgment Day, from Genesis to Revelation. It includes those believers from the Old Testament, the New Testament, the early church, the church in the present, and those who will believe in Christ until He returns on the Last Day. But this also means that "without the resurrection of Jesus there is no church, *ever* (past, present, future)!"

Even in the Old Testament, the prophecies of the Messiah pointed toward the resurrection. The first Gospel (*protoevangelium*) to Adam and Eve (Genesis 3:15) promised that the head of the serpent (Satan) would be crushed through the Seed of the woman. The devil's sowing of sin and death would be destroyed by the crucified and resurrected Christ. He would be born of a woman, born God and man under the Law to redeem those decimated by Eve's and Adam's fall (Galatians 4:4). This Messiah would come through Abraham's offspring and would be a blessing to all nations (Genesis 12:3). Abraham believed God's promises, and it was counted to him as righteousness (Genesis 15:6). This included God's call to sacrifice his own son, Isaac (Genesis 22:2), whom Abraham believed God could raise from the dead (Hebrews 11:17–19). Job, who may well have lived during the time of Abraham, also trusted in the resurrection through the coming Redeemer (Job 19:25–26). King David regularly expressed hope in the resurrection (Psalm 16:10; 17:15), which is based on the resurrection of the Messiah (Psalm 21:4; 22:21–31). Isaiah looked to the resurrection (Isaiah 25:8;

26:19), which would happen because the Messiah would rise (Isaiah 53:10). Ezekiel's vision of the valley of dry bones, which come to life according to God's Word (Ezekiel 37:1–14), points to the resurrection of the dead. And Daniel's prophecy of the Son of Man (Daniel 7:13–14) tells of the God-man, Jesus Christ, who would establish an everlasting kingdom; through His rising from the dead, the resurrection of all flesh on the Last Day is possible (Daniel 12:2). Hosea (13:14) predicts the destruction of death, pointing to Paul's words in 1 Corinthians 15:55–57. So throughout the Old Testament, we see that the promise of the resurrection of all flesh is made possible by the resurrection of the coming Messiah. The church (the true believers) of the Old Testament was saved by trusting in these promises that pointed to the resurrection of the Messiah.

As noted from 1 Corinthians 15, the apostle Paul links our forgiveness and salvation to Christ's resurrection. It is this forgiveness which makes us members of Christ's church and makes possible our own bodily resurrection on the Last Day. This is also identified elsewhere in the New Testament. Our justification (being declared righteous through the forgiveness of sins) is connected to Christ's resurrection (Romans 4:25). Our resurrection is coupled with Christ's resurrection by the Holy Spirit, who was involved in Jesus' resurrection and who dwells in us and who will raise us from the dead (Romans 8:11). Elsewhere, St. Paul says that we are new creatures in Christ because of our Lord's resurrection (2 Corinthians 5:15–17). The apostle Peter states that we are born again to a living hope because of the resurrection of Jesus Christ (1 Peter 1:3).

So how does this justification, forgiveness, and the Holy Spirit come to poor, miserable sinners? Again, the apostle Paul makes this clear:

> But now the righteousness of God has been manifested apart from the law, although the Law and the Prophets bear witness to it—the righteousness of God through faith in Jesus Christ for all who believe. For there is no distinction: for all have sinned and fall short of the glory of God, and are justified by His grace as a gift, through the redemption that is in Christ Jesus, whom God put forward as a propitiation by His blood, to be received by faith. (Romans 3:21–25)

This faith in Jesus Christ, by which we cling to God's Gospel promises and receive justification, forgiveness of sins, and eternal salvation, comes to us through means. Article V of the Augsburg Confession explains:

> So that we may obtain this faith, the ministry of teaching the Gospel and administering the Sacraments was instituted. Through the Word and Sacraments, as through instruments, the Holy Spirit is given [John 20:22]. He works faith, when and where it pleases God [John 3:8], in

> those who hear the good news that God justifies those who believe that they are received into grace for Christ's sake. This happens not through our own merits, but for Christ's sake. (AC V)

The apostle Paul and the creeds of the church connect Christ's resurrection to our forgiveness and to our membership in the Holy Christian Church. This forgiveness comes to us through faith in Jesus Christ as our Lord and Savior, and this faith comes to us through the means of grace, which are also called the marks of the church. Through the Gospel of Jesus' death and resurrection the Holy Spirit is given, and He works faith so that we trust that what Jesus accomplished by His life, death, and resurrection is both true and for us.

In the Nicene Creed, what Jesus accomplished is also linked to "one Baptism for the remission of sins." St. Paul tells us that in Holy Baptism we are joined to Christ's death and resurrection (Romans 6:3–5; Colossians 2:12). Peter announces that in Baptism we receive the forgiveness of sins and the Holy Spirit (Acts 2:38) and that Baptism now saves us (1 Peter 3:21). Furthermore, in our Lord's Supper, Jesus gives us His very crucified and resurrected body and blood in, with, and under bread and wine for the forgiveness of sins (1 Corinthians 11:23–25; Matthew 26:28). This sacrament also points to our resurrected Lord's return on the Last Day (1 Corinthians 11:26). Both Baptism and the Sacrament of the Altar connect us to Jesus' death and resurrection and bring us the forgiveness of sin.

The Word and Sacraments then make us members of the Holy Christian Church through faith in Jesus' life, death, and resurrection. This connection is further identified in Article VII of the Augsburg Confession: "Our churches teach that one holy Church is to remain forever. The Church is the congregation of saints [Psalm 149:1] in which the Gospel is purely taught and the Sacraments are correctly administered."

But without the resurrection of Jesus, there would be no church because there would be no forgiveness of sins, no means of grace, no Gospel message and sacraments, and thus no true faith that would thereby sanctify us and incorporate us into the Body of Christ, the church. As Paul said, if Christ be not raised, our faith would be futile (see 1 Corinthians 5:17).

Thanks be to God that this is not the case—not at all!

> But in fact Christ has been raised from the dead, the firstfruits of those who have fallen asleep. For as by a man came death, by a man has come also the resurrection of the dead. For as in Adam all die, so also in Christ shall all be made alive. . . . The sting of death is sin, and the power of sin is the law. But thanks be to God, who gives us the victory through our Lord Jesus Christ. (1 Corinthians 15:20–22, 56–57)

Christ is risen! He is risen indeed! Alleluia! Therefore, there is forgiveness, the Gospel is proclaimed, and the sacraments are administered. The Holy Spirit works faith and connects us to the Holy Christian Church, and God will on the Last Day raise us with glorified bodies unto life everlasting.

Endnotes

1 SC II (*LSCE*, 17–18).

2 C. F. W. Walther, *The Church and the Office of The Ministry*, ed. Matthew C. Harrison (St. Louis: Concordia Publishing House, 2012), 9.

THE LORD'S HEAVENLY KINGDOM

Timothy P. Mueller

PASTORS are not supposed to have favorites, but Martin was especially precious to me. He loved Jesus, loved his church, and loved his pastor. He prayed for me daily. When poor hearing kept him from enjoying group Bible study, he asked me to bring him Bible studies to do at home. When he was no longer able to attend worship, he treasured the Word and Sacrament of Jesus that I brought him. He missed his dear wife of sixty-two years, who had preceded him in death. One day he asked, "Pastor, I know that when Jesus returns, her body will be raised unto eternal life. But what is it like for her now? What does the Bible say about that?" I responded by loaning him a volume of Dr. Francis Pieper's *Christian Dogmatics*. I bookmarked the short chapter called "The State of Souls between Death and Resurrection,"[1] which is about the intermediate state, the theological term for the condition of a person after death but before Jesus raises the body on the Last Day. He found great comfort in the clear scriptural teaching on this topic.

It is a topic we approach with great humility. We are speaking of things totally unknown to us. How can soul and body be torn apart so that the soul is alive with Christ even as the body is dead in the earth? What happens when time-bound creatures enter eternity? We need the modesty of Paul. When describing how he was caught up into paradise, he says he does not even understand how it happened: "Whether in the body or out of the body I do not know, God knows" (2 Corinthians 12:2). Many Scriptures promise future blessings, but not every passage specifies whether we begin to enjoy them upon death or must wait until our resurrection on the Last Day. The topic calls for charity toward others who apply a passage differently. There are many questions to which we simply answer: "I do not know, God knows."

In paradise, Paul heard "things that cannot be told, which man may not utter" (2 Corinthians 12:4).

Yet in Scripture the Spirit has clearly revealed to us the unseen, unheard, unimaginable (1 Corinthians 2:9–10). What does He tell us?

"His Heavenly Kingdom" (2 Timothy 4:18)

At the end of his life, Paul wrote confidently to Timothy: "The Lord will rescue me from every evil deed and bring me safely into His heavenly kingdom. To Him be the glory forever and ever. Amen" (2 Timothy 4:18). Here is a good scriptural name for the intermediate state: the "Lord's heavenly kingdom." Paul was confident that even if Caesar would cut off his head, his soul would be safe in heaven with Jesus, who is King over all.

Truly with Jesus in Paradise (Luke 23:39–43)

Many people facing death have treasured the words of Jesus to the repentant thief on the cross. After rebuking the other thief, he said, "Jesus, remember me when You come into Your kingdom" (Luke 23:42). This opened a perfect opportunity for Jesus to talk about the resurrection on the Last Day. Jesus could well have responded, "When I come again in My kingdom, you will awaken from the dust and enjoy eternal life with Me" (see Daniel 12:2). Instead, however, Jesus the Good Shepherd/Pastor says, "Truly, I say to you, today you will be with Me in paradise" (Luke 23:43).

These are powerful words. "Truly" (literally "amen") emphasizes what He is about to say: "Take this seriously! This is My solemn promise!" "Today" tells us that it would come true immediately upon death. His soul was not doomed to wander the earth until he had made restitution for all that he had stolen. No, Jesus pardoned him completely. "You will be with Me" indicates much more than close proximity to Jesus. It indicates a bond, a fellowship, with Him. And "paradise" is a Persian term for an aristocrat's private park.[2] In His message to the church at Ephesus, Jesus says the tree of life is in the paradise of God (Revelation 2:7). We will be with Jesus there.

Philipp Nicolai served as pastor in Unna, Westphalia (Germany), during the terrible plague of 1597. In a brief time, 1,400 people from the village died. He lost many of his closest relatives and even some from his own home. As he sought to minister to the many dying and grieving, he searched the Scriptures and found great delight in its teaching about eternal life, not just after the resurrection but also immediately upon death. Concerning Jesus' promise to the repentant thief, Nicolai says:

> The souls of the elect continue after their departure from this world in the heavenly paradise and there lead a true life of paradise. . . . For this reason I heartily believe and hereby confess orally and in writing that the souls of the elect are not snuffed out like a light nor do they dissolve like thin air or a vapor nor lie snoring and sleeping until the Last Day . . . but that they live and that their life is a peaceful life, full of all comfort and every heavenly pleasure, and that this life begins after death, as Christ says to the thief: "Today you will be with Me in paradise." A dying Christian ought to make use of these words and learn well to extend and expand them: " 'Today, today,' says the Son of God, as if He would say, not only on the Last Day shall your life of paradise begin, but even today, in one or three or four hours, as soon as you die and the soul is separated from your body. Then your soul will not snore and sleep, nor remain straying and wandering between heaven and earth, but will be at once with Me in paradise and enjoy the glory, joy, and life of paradise with Me."[3]

Depart and Be with Christ, a Gain Far Better (Philippians 1:21–23)

The imprisonment of Paul could have ended either in his release, which would have meant more fruitful labor for him (Philippians 1:22), or in his execution, which was "gain" (Philippians 1:21). Which would be better? He says, "My desire is to depart and be with Christ, for that is far better" (Philippians 1:23).

Another powerful promise! Death means "departing" from this present life. Even as the body sleeps in the dust of the earth, the soul leaves behind all the tears of this present, fallen world (Revelation 7:17). Thankfully, when we die we no longer know what is going on here in this vale of tears (Isaiah 63:16). As I tell my congregations, "When I die, don't expect my soul to hover around and watch over you and be there to help you. No way! I'm out of here! Jesus will be with you (Matthew 28:20). He will send His holy angels to guard you (Psalm 91:11–12). You won't need me. My work on earth will be finished!"

Life with Christ in His heavenly kingdom will be "far better" than the life we have here. Through the means of grace, Christ gives huge blessings already in this life. Not one of those blessings will be lessened in the heavenly kingdom. If anything, they will be augmented; there will be only "gain" and no loss:

- *Justification/Forgiveness of Sins.* "For all have sinned and fall short of the glory of God, and are justified by His grace as a gift, through the redemption that is in Christ Jesus, whom God put forward as a propitiation [atoning sacrifice] by His blood, to be received by faith" (Romans 3:23–25). As a result, "we have peace with God through our Lord Jesus Christ" (Romans 5:1), and "there is therefore now no condemnation for those who are in Christ Jesus" (Romans 8:1). We can be certain that after we die there will be no punishment for the soul of any believer in Christ. There is no sin to be paid for, no suffering required. Jesus, in both body and soul, suffered all our punishment in our place (Matthew 26:38). By His resurrection from the dead, we are justified, pardoned, declared innocent (Romans 4:25). Because the Father did not spare His own Son, but gave Him up for us all, God is *for us* and not *against us* and nothing—not even death—will be able to separate us from His love (Romans 8:31–32, 38–39).

- *Security in His Hand.* "My sheep hear My voice, and I know them, and they follow Me. I give them eternal life, and they will never perish, and no one will snatch them out of My hand" (John 10:27–28). This security will only increase when we die.
- *Fellowship with God.* Jesus promised: "I am the vine; you are the branches. Whoever abides in Me and I in him, he it is that bears much fruit, for apart from Me you can do nothing" (John 15:5). Now Christ speaks to us in His Word, and we boldly speak to the Father in Jesus' name. Should we expect anything less in Christ's heavenly kingdom?

Because of this promise of augmented life with Christ when we die, many faithful Christians have said with Paul: "We would rather be away from the body and at home with the Lord" (2 Corinthians 5:8). We both take comfort in being with Jesus immediately in paradise and look forward to the "redemption of our bodies" on the Last Day (Romans 8:23). Paul, who desired to be with Christ in His heavenly kingdom (Philippians 1:23), also awaited the return of "the Lord Jesus Christ, who will transform our lowly body to be like His glorious body" (Philippians 3:20–21). It is not a matter of either/or; it is both/and. A good funeral sermon uses both to comfort a family whose loved one has died in Christ.

Eternal life in Christ is simply a matter of "good, better, best," as summarized in the LCMS 1991 Explanation of the Small Catechism (Question 190):

God gives eternal life to me and all believers in Christ.

A. Eternal life is a present possession. [See John 17:3 and John 3:36.]

B. At the time of death, the soul of a believer is immediately with Christ in heaven. [See Ecclesiastes 12:7 and Luke 23:43.]

C. At the Last Day the believers, in both body and soul, will begin the full enjoyment of being with Christ forever. [See 1 Corinthians 15:51–52 and 1 John 3:2.][4]

"Blessed Are the Dead . . . That They May Rest from Their Labors." (Revelation 14:13)

"And I heard a voice from heaven saying, 'Write this: Blessed are the dead who die in the Lord from now on.' 'Blessed indeed,' says the Spirit, 'that they may rest from their labors, for their deeds follow them!' " (Revelation 14:13). To be "blessed" is to be in a happy state as a recipient of divine favor. "Rest" is a rich biblical term that is not to be confused with "sleep." The dead in Christ are said to "sleep" because their lifeless *bodies* will one day awaken again when Christ calls them (see Mark 5:39–41; John 11:11, 43–44; 1 Thessalonians 4:13–18). The land of Israel had "rest" after the Lord delivered His people from their enemies (Joshua 21:43–44; 23:1; 2 Samuel 7:1). "Rest" comes to the desperate widow when she finds security in the home of a husband who cares for her (Ruth 1:9; 3:1). Here and now, through the forgiveness of sins, Jesus gives rest for our souls (Matthew 11:28–30).

We look for even better rest in His heavenly kingdom. All the struggles, warfare, and conflict will be in the past. No more roaring lion; no more rebellious, sinful flesh; no more influence from the wicked world. Here, we take up the sword of the Spirit to fight the good fight. There, they rest securely in the victory that Christ, their Bridegroom, gave them. There is no longer any possibility of falling away from Him; they are "the spirits of the righteous made perfect" (Hebrews 12:23). The works they did on earth were not in vain (1 Corinthians 15:58). Their good works that gave glory to God on earth (Matthew 5:16) accompany their souls into paradise and glorify Him there. Because God prepared them beforehand (Ephesians 2:10), they have lasting significance, unlike sins committed in this life, which are remembered no more.

"How Long . . . ?" (Revelation 6:10)

Not everything is complete for the souls in Christ's heavenly kingdom:

> I saw under the altar the souls of those who had been slain for the word of God and for the witness they had borne. They cried out with a loud voice, "O Sovereign Lord, holy and true, how long before You will

> judge and avenge our blood on those who dwell on the earth?" Then they were each given a white robe and told to rest a little longer, until the number of their fellow servants and their brothers should be complete, who were to be killed as they themselves had been. (Revelation 6:9–11)

The martyrs echo the lament uttered by so many on this side of heaven: "How long?" They eagerly await the last judgment, when Christ will right every wrong, including the murders inflicted on them. They are told to rest a little while longer until the full number of martyrs should be complete.

The intermediate state is not yet a state of perfection. God is not yet finished with these saints. There yet remains the completion of the church's mission on earth, the final judgment, and the resurrection of the body. Their bodies have not yet experienced Christ's victory over death, the last enemy to be destroyed (1 Corinthians 15:26). The Son has not yet restored creation and turned it all over to the Father and said, in effect, "Mission accomplished!" (see 1 Corinthians 15:25–28).

Here we see that the souls in paradise, even though they do not know the specifics of happenings on earth (Isaiah 63:16), do speak to God. Our Lutheran Confessions rightly say: "We admit that, just as the saints (when alive) pray for the Church universal in general, so in heaven they pray for the Church in general" and "Granted, the blessed Mary prays for the Church" (Ap XXI 9, 27). And we have no command or promise to pray to them, because Jesus alone is the mediator between God and human beings (1 Timothy 2:5).

"A Great Multitude . . . Coming out of the Great Tribulation." (Revelation 7:9–17)

The hymns and liturgy of the church have long recognized that the church triumphant is in existence now, even before the resurrection on the Last Day. Jesus shows John a great multitude in white robes, with palm branches in their hands, crying out to God: "Salvation belongs to our God who sits on the throne, and to the Lamb!" (Revelation 7:10). He is told: "These are the ones coming out of the great tribulation. They have washed their robes and made them white in the blood of the Lamb" (Revelation 7:14). They are not the ones who *have* come out of the great tribulation—as though they were all raised from the dead already—but the ones who *are coming* out of this vale of tears. One by one they enter the presence of Christ Himself.

Our songs of praise on earth join with the voices of the angels, the cherubim and seraphim, the "glorious company of the apostles," the "goodly fellowship of the prophets," and "the noble army of martyrs" (*LSB*, p. 223). When we partake of the Lord's Supper, we laud and magnify the glorious name of God, joining with "angels and archangels, and with all the company of heaven" including "Mary Magdalene, Peter and John, and with all the witnesses of the resurrection."[5] By virtue of our mutual connection to Christ, we saints on earth enjoy the "mystic sweet communion with those whose rest is won" (*LSB* 644:5). Indeed, we have drawn near, very near, to "the spirits of the righteous made perfect" (Hebrews 12:23). "Oh, blest communion, fellowship divine! We feebly struggle, they in glory shine; yet all are one in Thee, for all are Thine" (*LSB* 677:4).

It was very important to my brother Herb that his book trumpeting the resurrection of the body—both Christ's and ours—also include a chapter on the intermediate state. After he died, his dear wife, Faith, shared the death announcement that he, with great difficulty, had dictated to her about a week before his death:

> Please tell them: Herb is not here. Herb is with Jesus. Jesus came for him on [March 21, 2020]. He is now waiting for the general resurrection from the dead. Do not worry, he is safe. The Lord has delivered him from every evil of body and soul. The Lord has delivered him into His heavenly kingdom just as He will also deliver you and all who trust in Him (1 Corinthians 15:51–58 and 2 Timothy 4:18). Do not grieve as those who have no hope, but remember Jesus' promise for each of us: "Whoever comes to Me I will never cast out, for this is the will of My Father that I should lose nothing of all He has given Me but raise them up on the last day" (see John 6:39–40). And Jesus is alive today to do exactly that! For He said, "I am the resurrection and the life. Whoever believes in Me, though he die, yet shall he live, and everyone who lives and believes in Me shall never die" (John 11:25–26). The last trumpet will sound, and Jesus will meet us to take us to the new heavens and the new earth where every tear will be wiped away and death will be no more, and we shall always be with the Lord (Revelation 21–22).

Endnotes

1 Francis Pieper, *Christian Dogmatics*, trans. Walter W. F. Albrecht (St. Louis: Concordia Publishing House, 1953), 3:511–15.

2 See commentary note on 2 Corinthians 12:3 in *The Lutheran Study Bible*: "This Persian term for an aristocrat's private park became a loanword in intertestamental Judaism to describe first the Garden of Eden and then the dwelling place of believing souls after death. Some Jewish interpreters held that God took Eden to heaven."

3 Philipp Nicolai, *The Joy of Eternal Life*, trans. Matthew Carver (St. Louis: Concordia Publishing House, 2021), 208.

4 *Luther's Small Catechism with Explanation* (St. Louis: Concordia Publishing House, 1991), 166–67.

5 *Lutheran Service Book: Altar Book* (St. Louis: Concordia Publishing House, 2006), 232.

DEFENDING THE FAITH
FAITH FITS THE FACTS

The original source of the doubts that trouble our minds is the one who, from the beginning, has been asking, "Did God really say?" Yet knowing Jesus has defeated the devil, Christians trust there is no way "the gates of hell" (Matthew 16:18) can prevail against His church. We do not have to retreat in the face of any "new atheists." We can have courage in our witness. The atheist cannot answer a simple question: Why is there something rather than nothing? The Christian faith is not contrary to fact, but actually fits the facts better than a materialist view. The Word of the cross and the resurrection of Jesus both call us to account before God and provide the resolution to our deepest problems. This is all because the resurrection of Jesus actually happened. The message of the cross, while foolishness to the unbelieving world, is, because Jesus lives, the power of God for salvation for everyone who believes. St. Paul explains: "We preach Christ crucified, a stumbling block to Jews and folly to Gentiles, but to those who are called, both Jews and Greeks, Christ the power of God and the wisdom of God. For the foolishness of God is wiser than men, and the weakness of God is stronger than men" (1 Corinthians 1:23–25).

The bodily resurrection of Jesus Christ from the dead must be the heart of our defense for the hope that is within us. This was true in the first century. It will be true in the twenty-first century. Christianity is not primarily a matter of moral behavior, though we do speak of Christian morals, but Christianity is about Christ, crucified for our sins and bodily raised from the dead according to the eyewitness testimony of Scripture. Without Christ, without His life, His death in our place, His resurrection, His ascension to the right hand of God, and His imminent return to rescue us, there is no church, no Christian faith. This might seem obvious in the extreme, but we must be clear about it. We are convinced Christ Jesus, the eternal Son of the Father, true God and true man, is God's final and complete revelation of Himself in this world. We have come to know that His life and His death on the cross are the final and complete payment for the sins of the world—mine, yours, and everyone's. Christ made perfect satisfaction before God for all sinners. How do we know? Of this God "has given assurance to all by raising Him [Jesus] from the dead" (Acts 17:31).

Rev. Dr. Herbert C. Mueller Jr.

OBJECTIONS TO THE RESURRECTION[1]

Scott R. Murray

HOW can we be sure that we shall be raised incorruptible with Christ? Perhaps no doctrine of the Christian Gospel has been so universally criticized, mocked, and rejected than the doctrine of the bodily resurrection. Augustine says, "In nothing is the Christian faith so spoken against as in the resurrection of the flesh."[2] Of course, that mockery finds its expression already in Acts 17 in Paul's speech to the Athenian Areopagus, which seemed to be going swimmingly until he spoke of Christ as the righteous man who had been raised from the dead (Acts 17:31). This contention generated guffaws: "Now when they heard of the resurrection of the dead, some mocked. But others said, 'We will hear you again about this' " (Acts 17:32). As far as we know, Paul never received a return invitation, since the Greek mind considered the resurrection of the flesh less than ideal. The people of our time are not the first to deny the resurrection of the flesh and to mock it.

Luther points out that the resurrection of the dead is neither more nor less likely than any of the other central articles of the Christian doctrine: Baptism, absolution, the incarnation, or the real presence.[3] How could we have the courage to mock the resurrection, as did the Sadducees and the liberals of a previous generation?

Why are we Christians so sure of the bodily resurrection? God expressly wills that we should live forever in perfect fellowship with Him through our resurrection from the dead. Our Lord Jesus confounded the Sadducees, who denied the resurrection of the dead, when He pointed out that God names Himself with the names of His people: "As for the resurrection of the dead, have you not read what was said to you by God: 'I am the God of Abraham, and the God of Isaac, and the God of Jacob'? He is not God of the dead, but of the living" (Matthew 22:31–32). Notice that Jesus, when He quotes Scripture to His opponents, says that He is quoting God. He stuns the Sadducees by flatly rejecting their denial of the resurrection of the dead: "You are wrong, because you know neither the Scriptures nor the power of God" (Matthew 22:29). God's revealed will was that He should raise the dead.

God raised Jesus from the dead. That alone does not yet prove that we shall be raised. However, God revealed in His Word that the resurrection of Christ is the paradigm for all those who believe in Him. As Johann Gerhard put it, Christ's resurrection "is not only an example, prelude, earnest and pledge but also the efficient cause and source of our own resurrection."[4] The cause assuring us that we are possessors of eternal life is Christ's own triumphant resurrection. "For if we have been united with Him in a death like His, we shall certainly be united with Him in a resurrection like His" (Romans 6:5). Jesus Himself says, "Because I live, you also will live" (John 14:19). When Jesus says, "I am the resurrection and the life" (John 11:25), this statement is not merely a statement of raw fact, but it also has salvific effect for us. Jesus is saying, "Not only shall I Myself rise again and live, but I shall also be the cause of resurrection and life for others."[5] Jesus subsequently demonstrates His power over death by raising Lazarus from his tomb in that graveyard.

Jesus demonstrated His power over death during His public ministry by raising the dead. At the resurrection of Lazarus, Jesus strolls into the boneyard to put flesh and bone back in order (John 11:38; Ezekiel 37). Why? Because He is the Lord God of Israel, who gives life and takes it away, who kills and makes alive. The enemy thinks he has barred His way. The tomb is slammed shut. Jesus has even given death a head start, so He can assure us and all His disciples that death cannot hold Him, the tomb cannot remain shut against Him.

He confronts even Martha's sensible, if ghoulish, undertaker's warning, "Lord, he stinks." It is as though He said to her: "Yes, I know what decomposition is. I know what condition Lazarus is in." Maybe you have had that quiet moment before the casket of a loved one, when death seemed to be ascendant over life. My mother and I shared that moment at the side of my father's casket. That moment when she reached in to touch the hand of a beloved husband. Tear-washed eyes met over the casket, and she said, "He's cold." Mary and Martha knew that feeling: "He's cold and decaying, Jesus."

But what is that to the Life of all the living? Why should death stand in His way? What power has the stink of putrefaction against the true incense of life? The sweet-smelling odor of the offering to the Father must take away the stink of death. It does by calling forth life from death. In Him we become the fragrance of life (2 Corinthians 2:16).

Let us then offer up the sweet odor of faith and life in the graveyard of death. How ought we to pray for those who need the Lord's life, those who doubt God's power over death and its decay? We shall speak the stink to silence. Our decaying bodies weighed down by age, trouble, and death have come to hear Jesus say, "Come forth," a word first spoken in Baptism and at the last repeated on the day of resurrection.

The raising of Lazarus tells us that there is no reason why the graveyard must stay full. The God who comes to the graveyard of the world comes to say to our corpse: "Lazarus, come out." Even (and especially) COVID-19 cannot change the power of Christ over death. Jesus asks us, "Did I not tell you that if you believed you would see the glory of God?" (John 11:40). Is He not still asking us believers the same question? Are we not listening? Can we not say, "Yes, Jesus, You did!"?

Our dying accomplishes the good that comes from the life of Christ. This is what is happening when we give ourselves up to one another in humble and sacrificial repentance, saying, "Dear brother, dear sister, I have sinned against you. I have transgressed against your person. Please forgive me. I have done you wrong." We might well weep tears of grief because this is so humiliating, yet with us, Jesus weeps. When we are living in Baptism by repenting, we are truly living while we are dying.

I am praying to let Jesus' life come through my death. Jesus let life come through His death. Let life live. You can live in dying. Jesus assures us: "Whoever believes in Me, though he die, yet shall he live, and everyone who lives and believes in Me shall never die" (John 11:25–26).

We need to let Christ perish, or we shall. God must die, or we will not live. The trade-off is quite simple. There can be no new life without death. If the old dying life is not done to death, there will not be the immortal life conferred through it. We are dying to live, just as Lazarus did.

The devil was overcome by that through which he held power. Through that weapon—that is, death—which was his strength against the world, Jesus crushed him. See what a great blessing death has worked. Why, then, do you tremble? Why are you afraid of death? It is no longer terrifying. It has been trodden underfoot. It has been despised and smashed by Jesus. You, too, should despise it because Jesus has. Luther says:

> This is also the way a Christian can defy death: "Although I must be buried beneath the earth and become ashes, I have the Lord above, who is of my flesh and blood, who will never die again (Rom. 6:9), because

> He is utterly alive. He became my Lord so that I might not remain in the power of death or the devil. I shall live with Him. I believe that death cannot strangle life as much as Christ can give life. And He will give even more. Thus also St. Paul writes (Rom. 14:8–9): 'Whether we are dead or alive, we belong to the Lord. For to this end He died and rose again that He might be Lord both of the dead and of the living.' Therefore, even though I must die, I shall nonetheless live, because my Lord lives, who was Lord also in death. He shall not leave me in death, but as He lives, so I shall live also. As He says Himself: 'I live, and you shall live also' (John 14:19); or 'Where I am, there shall My servant be also' (John 12:26)." (AE 13:244–45)

Christ's resurrection gives us certainty about our own. Just as He was laid in the grave, so, too, will we be. Just as He burst death's doors, so we shall burst forth from death unto life. It must be this way, just as the head is always followed by the body. If the head rises, so also will the body. We are that body that follows the Head from the grave. Here is why there is such great joy in the Easter season for us Christians: because it proclaims not just the Lord's indestructible life, but it also teaches us our own. So connected is our resurrection to Christ's that Luther can say:

> For our Lord Jesus Christ began the resurrection in His own body, but the resurrection is not completed unless we, too, are raised. . . . Therefore, after the resurrection of Christ, one must preach about our own resurrection, since the two belong together in order that the resurrection may be complete. (AE 58:102)

So certain are we of this life in Christ that for us death is only a "little sleep." Jesus describes the dead maiden (Mark 5:39) and His friend Lazarus (John 11:11–12) as only asleep because they will rise. Paul is so certain of this awakening that he does not speak of us as the "dead" but only as those who are asleep (1 Corinthians 15:18–20). I am just as certain that I will rise from the bed of death as I am that I will awaken tomorrow morning after a peaceful night of sleep. This is why we pray, "Now I lay me down to sleep . . . ."

The raising of Tabitha, Lazarus, and the son of the widow all assure us that Christ has the power of life in His hands and therefore can fulfill His promise to be our resurrection and life. The Gospel of St. Matthew also presents us with those who rose with Christ and after coming into the Jerusalem below testified to the Jerusalem above: "The tombs also were opened. And many bodies of the saints who had fallen asleep were raised, and coming out of the tombs after His resurrection they went into the holy city and appeared to many" (Matthew 27:52–53). The resurrection of Christ showed its shared nature when the tombs of those around Him could not remain occupied at

His rising. The empty tombs of Easter were a stunning anticipation of what is yet to come for us.

What does Jesus say about the resurrection? Jesus teaches a bodily resurrection. He warns us not to fear those who kill the people who confess Him: "Do not fear those who kill the body but cannot kill the soul. Rather fear Him who can destroy both soul and body in hell" (Matthew 10:28). The obvious parallel to this threat is the clear implication of the promise that the believer will be saved both body and soul in heaven. As Tertullian argued on the basis of this text: "Since, then, the body after the resurrection has to be killed by God in hell along with the soul, we surely have sufficient information in this fact respecting both the issues *which await it*, namely the resurrection of the flesh, and its eternal 'killing.'"[6] The resurrection will certainly be a body-and-soul event, both for good and for ill.

Jesus directly teaches a universal resurrection and, therefore, a resurrection of both believers and unbelievers:

> Truly, truly, I say to you, an hour is coming, and is now here, when the dead will hear the voice of the Son of God, and those who hear will live. For as the Father has life in Himself, so He has granted the Son also to have life in Himself. And He has given Him authority to execute judgment, because He is the Son of Man. Do not marvel at this, for an hour is coming when all who are in the tombs will hear His voice and come out, those who have done good to the resurrection of life, and those who have done evil to the resurrection of judgment. (John 5:25–29)

First, the cause of the resurrection of believers is the life-giving voice of the Son of God that awakens them from their graves. He confers life because He is the life. Second, there are those who will be raised to judgment because they have done evil.

Is the resurrection worked by Christ really a bodily resurrection? Who are the dead of which Paul speaks in 1 Corinthians 15? In many ancient texts, "the dead" is used for a corpse, that is, the body of a dead person. Greg Lockwood, in his commentary on this text, says, "The term νεκρὸς [dead] often carries graphic realism. Christ's resurrection—and the believer's—is the real, physical resurrection of their bodies."[7] Given this, Lockwood argues that the term "resurrection of the dead" could easily be translated as "resurrection of corpses."[8]

If the early Christians were attempting to downplay or soften the resurrection of the dead in keeping with the well-known Greek aversion to a bodily resurrection, they did a poor job of it. Instead, the apostles stubbornly used the term "the dead" to refer to the condition of the resurrected, even in the face of its connection with corpses. The terms are put cheek by jowl no less than twenty-six times in the New Testament, four of those in 1 Corinthians alone. No, this is an emphatic avowal of a real, physical, bodily resurrection.

How is this body raised? Luther simply bats this back into the lap of the questioner by asking, "What makes you think that the almighty God, Creator of the universe, is incapable of such a thing?" For Luther, the denial of the bodily resurrection is tantamount to rank unbelief and a breach of the First Commandment.[9] No wonder Paul blasts the questioner of 1 Corinthians 15 with the epithet "Fool!" (1 Corinthians 15:36 KJV), for has not the fool said in his heart there is no God (Psalm 14:1)?

In our time, we stumble over Paul's adjective "spiritual," thinking it to be the opposite of physical, when in 1 Corinthians the opposite of "spiritual" is "natural" (ψυχικός; 1 Corinthians 2:14; 15:44, 46).[10] Note, too, that spiritual food and the spiritual Rock are both very real and physical (1 Corinthians 10:3–4).

Gregory Lockwood puts in conjunction the two emphases highlighted by Paul: "Paul's response stresses both the *continuity* of the resurrected body with the believer's earthly remains, and their remarkable *transformation* into a glorified, spiritual body."[11] Luther takes up this theme by saying:

> Man will retain only what pertains to his essence, but nothing will remain that relates to this transitory life. And yet it will be the same body and soul with all the members that man had here. But he will have to leave behind all that he required in this world. (AE 28:182)

If we look for an example of this spiritual body and if Christ is the firstfruits of the resurrection (1 Corinthians 15:20, 23), there is no more helpful and comforting example to prove His bodily and physical resurrection than the resurrected Christ who eats food (Luke 24:41–43), who points to His bodily wounds (John 20:27) in the presence of His disciples, and who was recognized by them, and yet is unconstrained by physical barriers (John 20:19). We, too, will be recognizable flesh and blood yet be truly spiritual. Now that is something to look forward to! We will continue dying until we will be raised up to the resurrected life at Christ's coming, a life like the resurrected Christ's life (Romans 6:1–11; 2 Corinthians 5:17; 1 Corinthians 15; etc.).

When the pastors who succeed me go to the deathbed of the people I catechized, what will they say? Their last words will be the first words that were set upon their heart and their forehead: "In the name of the Father and of the Son and of the Holy Spirit." "Dear Lord, now I go to see that which I only hoped for and believed and trusted my whole life. Now it's all mine." Baptism makes its return when the beginning and the end of the Christian life meet and kiss.[12]

Let us defy death by confessing the resurrection. During the COVID-19 pandemic, eleven people tested positive after attending Easter Sunday 2021 services at my parish. Everyone recovered quickly, except one elderly saint who spent about four weeks in the intensive care unit. While his wife was at home in quarantine, I kept in contact with her by phone, praying with her, comforting her and finding out how her husband was doing in the hospital. I apologized to her for the trial that she was undergoing because of their attendance at Easter Sunday service. Her husband was wavering between life and death. Despite that, she said, "Oh, pastor! It was all worth it to be able to attend Easter service with God's people." She knew what it meant to defy death. Her Lord was living, living for her and her husband.

Endnotes

1 This essay is based on the convention essay delivered to the Central Illinois District Convention and appears as "Baptism, Sanctification, and Resurrection," in *The 60th Regular Convention Central Illinois District Lutheran Church—Missouri Synod Proceedings* (2022), 26–52.

2 As quoted in Johann Gerhard, *On the Resurrection of the Dead and the Last Judgment*, Theological Commonplaces 30–31 (St. Louis: Concordia Publishing House, 2020), 9.

3 *Eastertide Sermons on 1 Corinthians 15* (AE 58:116): "And just as we must and should treat this article of the resurrection, so also should we treat the other articles of the Christian faith, whether of Baptism, Absolution, the Lord's Supper, etc. We should set reason entirely aside and say: 'If God has spoken it, then it will surely come to pass.'"

4 Gerhard, *On the Resurrection*, 17.

5 Gerhard, *On the Resurrection*, 57.

6 Tertullian, "The Resurrection of the Flesh," *ANF* 3:571.

7 Gregory Lockwood, *1 Corinthians*, Concordia Commentary (St. Louis: Concordia Publishing House, 2000), 559. Interestingly, what the ancients called a νεκροφέρος, we would call a "pall bearer," testifying to the source of life and the ultimate disposition of the bodily remains.

8 Lockwood, *1 Corinthians*, 562: "Is it really possible that this sin-filled, decayed flesh could be subject to the blessings of divine righteousness by the power of the Holy Spirit? Luther in his characteristic hyperbole calls the human body a bag of worms. We commonly call a buried corpse 'worm food.'" See Scott R. Murray, "Resurrection of the Flesh," in *You, My People, Shall Be Holy*, ed. John R. Stephenson and Thomas M. Winger (St. Catharines: Concordia Lutheran Theological Seminary, 2013), 153.

9 See Luther's 1544 Easter sermon in AE 58:102–18.

10 "*Psychikos* describes a state of life out of touch with God. Paul writes that the natural (*psychikos*) person cannot discern the things of God (1 Cor 2:14). Paul also

contrasts the spiritual, resurrected body with the natural (*psychikos*) body using the same term (1 Cor 15:44, 46)" (Joel T. Hamme, "Soul," in *Lexham Theological Wordbook*, ed. Douglas Mangum, Derek R. Brown, Rachel Klippenstein, and Rebekah Hurst, Lexham Bible Reference Series [Bellingham, WA: Lexham Press, 2014]).

11 Lockwood, *1 Corinthians*, 584, emphasis original.

12 See Gregory of Nazianzus, *Theological Orations* 40.15.

“DEAD MEN DON’T COME BACK. THEY STAY DEAD.” BUT WHAT IF?

Kirk M. Clayton

FOR many in our culture, the universe is all that ever was, is, and will be. This sentiment even found its way into the opening of Carl Sagan’s book *Cosmos* and, from it, into the opening narration for the *Cosmos* TV show that ran for thirteen episodes on PBS in 1980. This sentiment has shaped fifty years of our thought and, supported by one of the most respected scientists of the twentieth century, sounds official and indisputable. The implication is that we live in a constrained, naturalistic universe that runs independently of any outside force, and in fact there can be no outside force, since the universe is all that is. But what if that statement is wrong? What if it is dead wrong?

Many confuse the search for truth with the scientific method, often thinking of science as if it were the only method for determining facts and truth. A mere three and a half minutes into the first episode of *Cosmos*, Sagan claims that science deals with truth, and he promises that the show will clearly mark the difference between hypothesis and fact. The problem, however, is that the foundational underpinning of *Cosmos* (book and show)—that the universe is all that ever was, is, and will be—is not fact. It cannot be tested. Such a claim is a statement of philosophy, not science.

Let’s consider another claim: “Dead men don’t come back. They stay dead.” While it seems to be a claim of fact, a solid statement of science, this is also a speculative statement. This claim also is a statement of philosophy, not of science. This is a statement of a naturalistic outlook that denies the possibility of miracles. It presupposes that no resurrection has ever happened under any circumstance and that no resurrection could ever happen under any circumstance. The statement rules out any possibility of a resurrection before even bothering to test the hypothesis. No experimentation or testing is necessary because the statement simply assumes it is true. That is why it is a speculative statement, not a scientific one. The statement may be somewhat logical if "the cosmos is all that is or was or ever will be." However, since that statement about the cosmos itself is speculative and philosophical rather than scientific, the statement that "Dead men don't come back. They stay dead" is also speculative and philosophical.

These speculative, nonscientific statements are based on the idea that nature and the laws of nature are absolute and unchangeable. In this view, it is impossible to interfere with natural laws. This view is in error, or at least incomplete. True, we see the laws of nature at work all around us on a constant basis. However, while we do not often think in these terms, we also see outside forces acting on the laws of nature and constantly changing their effects as well.

Here is a simple example. We all are familiar with the legend that Sir Isaac Newton saw an apple fall from a tree and thus "discovered" gravity. Gravity has become a standard law of nature. In a simplified form, the law of gravity says that objects will be attracted to each other, and we know that the larger, more massive an object is, the greater its gravitational pull will be on objects around it. So an apple falling from a tree will be pulled to the earth, which is much more massive and has much stronger gravity. However, if I happen to be walking by the tree just as the apple falls, and I reach out my hand to catch the apple, it does not fall to the earth. I, an outside force, have intervened in the law of nature. This happens with great regularity.

To claim that miracles, including the resurrection, cannot occur without even testing the hypothesis is actually unscientific. What if we instead take an open, more scientific approach that relies on evidence and examination? What if we take the approach that any claim of a miracle should be given a thorough investigation before declaring out of hand that it is impossible? That is truly the more scientific position. It sets forth a theory and then seeks to test the theory and search for evidence to prove or disprove it.

Let's go back to our speculative statement "Dead men don't come back. They stay dead." What would it take to transform this from speculation to science? Test it out. Experiment. Rather than simply state the conclusion as a fact, subject the claim to the rigors of examination. Revise the statement to something such as this: "Dead men don't come back. They stay dead. But *what if*?" That question at the end, that "what if," opens the statement to exploration and experimentation. That question "what if" moves the statement from speculation to science.

So what if we examine the claim that Jesus actually did rise from the dead on Easter morning instead of automatically dismissing the claim by making the speculative statement that "Dead men don't come back. They stay dead"? Let's look at the evidence for the claim that Jesus rose and see where that examination leads us. As we put the claims of the resurrection of Jesus to the test, we will use two main forms of evidence. First, we will look at the evidence of the empty tomb of Jesus on Easter morning. Second, we will look at the evidence in the dramatic transformation we see in the lives of the apostles after the resurrection of Jesus.

Contrary to the predominant narrative regularly repeated by academics and pseudo-scientists, we have very strong historical evidence that the tomb where Jesus' dead body was laid on Good Friday was, in fact, empty on Easter morning. Now, we need to say up front that an empty tomb does not in itself prove a resurrection. However, it does open the door to the possibility of a resurrection, if no better explanations can be given. Rather than assuming that a resurrection could not take place, we need to examine the possibilities and determine which is the most likely explanation. First, we will consider the evidence for the empty tomb itself.

Here is the strongest evidence that Jesus' tomb was empty on Easter morning: even the chief priests, who desperately wanted Jesus to be and remain dead, had to admit that Jesus' tomb was empty. This is exactly what we see in Matthew's account of the resurrection. The soldiers who had been assigned to guard Jesus' tomb—specifically to make sure that Jesus' dead body stayed in the tomb—rushed to the chief priests to tell their strange story about an earthquake, angels, and the empty tomb. The chief priest instructed the flustered guards: "Tell people, 'His disciples came by night and stole Him away while we were asleep'" (Matthew 28:13). This is very enlightening. The best way for the chief priests to deny the resurrection would have been to deny that Jesus' tomb was empty and instead point to His dead, rotting body still wrapped in its grave clothes on its bench in the tomb. However, the chief priests instead had to instruct the soldiers to say that Jesus' disciples came and stole His body. There is only one plausible reason for this. The tomb of Jesus really was empty, and the chief priests knew it.

When the easiest answer that could be given is not given, especially when that easiest answer would also be the most advantageous answer, then it is a strong indication that something strange is going on. In this case, clearly the most advantageous answer for the chief priests would have that Jesus' body remained in His tomb. The chief priests had invested a lot of resources into having Jesus killed and had even taken steps specifically to ensure His body remained in the tomb. The fact that they could not point to His body in the tomb, even when it would be the easiest, most advantageous answer, is very strong evidence that Jesus' body was not in the tomb. So they had to resort to plan B. Jesus' tomb was empty, so they had to explain it away in the next best way. They came up with the story that Jesus' disciples came and stole His body.

This story is implausible on several levels. First, the story hinges on the soldiers falling asleep while on guard duty. In the Roman empire, the penalty for this offense was death. To buy into this story, one would have to believe that a group of well-trained soldiers, under penalty of death, all fell fast asleep and that they slept so soundly that they did not hear a grave robbery taking place. Remember that any one of the guards would likely have awakened at so much as the snap of a twig or the rustle of a leaf. Then remember that to gain access to the body, the disciples would have had to roll back the large stone in front of the tomb, which would have been a very noisy undertaking as stone grated against stone. It is completely implausible that the guards could have stayed asleep during such an undertaking. Second, think about the shame involved. The soldiers would have to admit that they had been bested by a Galilean gang of disorganized disciples with no military training. Oh, the embarrassment! And, finally, remember that soldiers were told to say that they had been sleeping while the whole event took place. And yet they could provide identification that the disciples were the culprits? Sleepers do not see anything and cannot identify anyone! The whole story is absurd. There is no way that Jesus' tomb was empty because His disciples stole His body while a group of guards were sleeping.

There was no way the tomb was empty because the disciples stole Jesus' body, but the tomb was empty! We need to continue to explore the reason why that could be. Other theories have been proposed to explain the empty tomb, since the "Stolen Body Theory" clearly does not hold up. These theories include the "Swoon Theory," the "Lettuce Theory," the "Twin Theory," and the "Wrong Tomb Theory." While I will not dive into these theories here, they are all orders of magnitude less plausible than even the "Stolen Body Theory." We can have great certainty that Jesus' tomb was empty on Easter morning, and there is only one plausible, or even possible, answer. Jesus rose from the dead. Dead men usually stay dead, but not in this case. The evidence indicates that this man, Jesus, did come back to life.

We also find convincing evidence of the resurrection of Jesus in the changed lives of His disciples. Prior to Jesus' resurrection, the disciples revealed themselves to be afraid of rejection and death, and they were determined to keep Jesus away from danger. When Jesus was arrested and His future looked bleak, all the disciples fled in fear. Even after the initial news of the resurrection, the disciples were still terrified, hiding behind locked doors. And yet, less than two months later these same disciples were boldly proclaiming Jesus as crucified and risen at the festival of Pentecost in Jerusalem, probably to some of the very people who had cried out "Crucify Him! Crucify Him!" only fifty days earlier (John 19:6). These same disciples continued to proclaim Jesus and His resurrection in Jerusalem even when they were told not to do so and even when they were imprisoned because of their proclamation.

Facing persecution and imprisonment, they still publicly preached Jesus. Throughout the next thirty to sixty years, these formerly fearful followers traveled the world to proclaim that Jesus had risen and defeated death. At nearly every turn they faced mockery, violence, arrests, and the threat of death. They did not become wealthy or famous because of their proclamation. In fact, they were impoverished and unpopular specifically because of their message of Jesus' death and resurrection. In the end, most likely all but one of the disciples was put to death because of the message that Jesus had defeated death. Even in the face of persecution and martyrdom, not one of them recanted his statements that Jesus had risen from the dead.

It has been said that nobody willingly dies for what they know to be a lie. People have certainly died for lies that they did not know about because they themselves were deceived. This usually happens when people are too distant from the subject to be adequately informed about it. However, the disciples based their proclamation of Jesus' resurrection on their own first-hand experience. They claimed that they had seen Jesus personally. They had heard Him. They had eaten with Him. They had touched Him. And then they suffered poverty, abuse, rejection, and death because of it. It would have been in the disciples' best interests to deny the resurrection. But they knew that if they would have done that, *then they would have been living a lie*, which would have resulted in a fate far worse than death. Instead, they held to what they knew beyond all shadow of a doubt to be the truth. Jesus did rise from the dead, and in doing so He had defeated death so that they also had nothing to fear. Death could not defeat Jesus, so death would not defeat them either. That is why they would willingly die for the proclamation of the resurrection.

For these reasons and others, the evidence for the resurrection of Jesus Christ is really very strong. In fact, the resurrection has been described as one of the most provable events in all of history. The evidence is there, just asking to be examined. That is what science does. It is unscientific to deny any possibility of a resurrection without examining the evidence. To make a blanket statement such as "Dead men don't come back. They stay dead" is to make not a scientific statement but a speculative statement that denies the possibility before any examination or exploration.

We could agree to the truth of the statement "Dead men *usually* don't come back. They *usually* stay dead." This statement is obviously true and can be tested. But *what if*? What if it really happened one time that a man really did come back from the dead? Ask the question and follow the evidence to the answer. What if someone really did come back from the dead? What if? Check it out!

JOY OF LIFE
NIGHTS OF GROANING

I have often reflected with other pastors that the pastoral ministry can become a daily struggle with sin and death. There is so much brokenness in the world. It shows up in families. It shows up in the behavior even of fellow Christians at times. We live in a fallen world, a world in which there is much brokenness. This is nowhere more evident than when a pastor is called to give pastoral care at a sudden death.

That Tuesday in July began innocently enough. It was late morning, and I was working on my sermon for the following Sunday. The phone rang: "Pastor, would you come? Johnny just died of a heart attack."

I went and brought comfort to the grieving family. The man who died was fifty-five years old. I was thirty-three at the time. So it seemed that it was a natural thing for a fifty-five-year-old to die of a sudden heart attack—not entirely unexpected.

I spent the afternoon and early evening with the family. As I arrived home about suppertime, my wife was waiting on the front porch of our house. "Here, Herb, you have to call this number. There's been a terrible accident." It turned out that a young man from our congregation had drowned on a youth canoe trip with the youth group of a neighboring congregation.

The upshot of it was that they could not find the young man's parents. No one was answering the telephone at their home. Now, this young man was the only son of his parents. They had five daughters whom they loved dearly, and then this one son. I knew where one of the daughters was, with her husband. So the three of us drove out to the farm where the family lived. We found the mother in the yard mowing the grass and found out that the father was at the far end of the farm. How do you tell a father that his only son is dead? There is no good way. Besides, when he sees the pastor's car coming toward him across the field, he has to know that something terrible has happened.

The whole family gathered in the farmyard in the gathering gloom. We sat on lawn chairs in a circle. Such grief. Such groaning. In the dark, we brought our grief before the Lord. We struggled. We groaned. We groaned especially with Romans 8:33: "Who shall bring any charge against God's elect?" One thing I learned that night was that this grieving family was not interested in Herb Mueller's opinion. They wanted to know what God has to say. And so we ran to every Scripture I knew that promised resurrection and return to life in Christ.

The next day I went with the parents to identify the body, which had been brought from the location of the canoe trip. I went with them to choose the casket, and we began to plan the funeral. That afternoon was the visitation for the first death that had occurred that week.

I decided that I needed to go see the family once more since more family members were coming in from a distance. Again, we sat in the yard in the warm July night, groaning our prayers, trusting the Word of God that the Spirit prays along with us, looking again and again to Jesus, who bodily rose from the dead and promises that we, too, shall rise. As Jesus promised: "This is the will of Him who sent Me, that I should lose nothing of all that He has given Me, but raise it up on the last day" (John 6:39).

I took my leave about 8:30 p.m. When I arrived home, again, my wife was waiting for me on the front porch of our house. "Herb, you have to go down to the hospital." Another young man of our congregation, about twenty-one years old, had been working under a house. He had come into contact with electricity and was electrocuted. They didn't know if he was going to live. As I was driving to the hospital, I remember pounding on the dashboard of my car, crying out to God, saying, "God, please let him live. I'm not sure I can deal with more death tonight." But when I arrived at the hospital, it became altogether too clear that this young man was dead as well. I was there until at least 1:00 a.m. with his mother and his brother, again crying out to God. But in our groaning, we were "looking to Jesus, the founder and perfecter of our faith, who for the joy that was set before Him endured the cross, despising the shame, and is seated at the right hand of the throne of God" (Hebrews 12:2).

There is no comfort other than the promised resurrection in Christ. Nothing else will do. Nothing else matters.

We had three funerals that week: one on Thursday, one on Friday, and one on Saturday. These were all well-known people in the congregation, and many people from the parish came to all three funerals.

On Sunday morning, the text happened to be Romans 8:28: "We know that for those who love God all things work together for good, for those who are called according to His purpose." I read the text and said, "Oh, yeah, even now. What could be worse than the Son of God lying dead and buried in a grave? But God brought good out of that by raising Him from the dead. So the resurrection of Jesus—the bodily resurrection of Jesus—is what guarantees this promise that God works all things for good. It does not say that all things are good, but it says that God works all things for good. Again, the bottom line is that the promise is guaranteed by the bodily resurrection of Jesus. For at every single funeral, we show the resurrection of the dead. We lay the bodies of our loved ones to rest in the grave. Earth to earth, ashes to ashes, and dust to dust. But we do so in the sure and certain hope of the resurrection to eternal life, looking to Jesus, 'who will transform our lowly body to be like His glorious body, by the power that enables Him even to subject all things to Himself' (Philippians 3:21)."

The main thing I learned that horrible week was that in the face of death, God's people were not interested at all in this young pastor's opinion. My opinion counted for nothing. The only thing that made a difference was the Word and promise of God. The only thing we had to hang on to was the fact that Jesus rose from the dead in victory over sin and death and the fact that He promises the same victory to us. When we say, "I believe in . . . the resurrection of the dead," we are speaking first of Jesus who was bodily raised from the dead, but then we are speaking also of Jesus' promise to raise us.

Rev. Dr. Herbert C. Mueller Jr.

THE RESURRECTION CHANGES EVERYTHING

William C. Weedon

And He said to me, "Son of man, can these bones live?" (Ezekiel 37:3)

THINK of the scene: Ezekiel walking among the bleached bones, strewn across the face of the valley. They had been people once. They had loved and laughed; they ate and drank; they danced and sang; and, yes, they fought and died. We call them "remains" because apparently they are all that is left of the life that once animated those bones. But the question put by the Lord to His prophet is *the* question, or almost the question. *Can these bones live?*

We obviously have no way to make them live again. We can put the bones under a microscope and answer questions about who they once were and even learn a bit of what they once ate. Depending on the marks on the bones, we might even be able to take a stab at the cause of death, though in Ezekiel's vision it certainly seems as if it was a horrid battle that left them all unburied and exposed to the elements and animals so that they were slowly wasting away. *Can these bones live?*

Although our study of these bones might glean a thing or two about their past, our studies yield no information about their future. There is nothing intrinsic in the bones that would suggest they might spring to life again. And going by human experience here upon earth, the solid answer to God's question surely is, *No, they cannot live again. The dead are dead and gone.*

But that is to reckon without the God of Israel, who is the *living* God, the God of life. And Ezekiel knows better than to ignore Him. So he gives what can only be regarded as the "safe" answer: "O Lord God, You know" (Ezekiel 37:3). Well, of course He does know. But His will is that His prophet would know and through him His people would know, so that they can be a people filled with this crazy hope that changes absolutely everything. So that the prophet and God's people might also know, he is instructed: "Prophesy over these bones, and say to them, O dry bones, hear the word of the LORD" (Ezekiel 37:4). And what is that word of the Lord spoken over these remains? Listen: "Thus says the Lord GOD to these bones: Behold, I will cause breath to enter you, and you shall live. And I will lay sinews on you, and will cause flesh to come upon you, and cover you with skin, and put breath in you, and you shall live, and you shall know that I am the LORD" (Ezekiel 37:5–6).

To bones that have no capacity to revive themselves comes life, a word from the Source of life, the very one who created life at the beginning: " 'Let there be . . .' and there was" (Genesis 1:3). And so the prophet sets about his divinely appointed task: to pronounce over dead bones a promise of life from the living God. And as he spoke, it began to happen. Bone to its bone, sinews wrapping round, flesh covering the innards, the nature of man reconstituted. It was a reminder in a way of Genesis 2 and the way God first formed man from the ground. But there was still a problem: they had gone from bone to corpse, but corpses they were still. It was a miracle. But the greater miracle was to come. Hence: "Prophesy to the breath; prophesy, son of man, and say to the breath, Thus says the Lord GOD: Come from the four winds, O breath, and breathe on these slain, that they may live" (Ezekiel 37:9). Again, at the bidding of his God, the prophet speaks. The Word performs what it says. And before Ezekiel's astonished and delighted eyes, they are all reanimated. They stand on their feet before him, breathing, a vast army. He has just seen a fast-forward rewind of death itself, and it left him gobsmacked with awe. *Can these bones live?* To borrow a line from our Master: "With man it is impossible, but not with God. For all things are possible with God" (Mark 10:27). Yes, even the dead are living and breathing again, alive again. But to know that God can do this is not yet fully the joy of the resurrection that changed all things. The question is not *can* He but *will* He?

Certainly, by the time of the New Testament, the Jewish faithful had been convinced by the power of God's Word (maybe especially from Job 19 and Isaiah 25) that God not only could but would do so. You can hear such faith ringing through Martha's plaintive cry: "I know that he [Lazarus] will rise again in the resurrection on the last day" (John 11:24). You can hear such faith in St. Paul's ingenious dividing of the council with the cry: "It is with respect to the hope and the resurrection of the dead that I am on trial" (Acts 23:6). Pharisees, you see, answered the question *Can these bones live?* with a firm, "Yes, and they will too!" Sadducees, however, were more like most people today: "Dead is dead is dead." Make no mistake about it, the

Jewish faithful by the time of the New Testament would happily have professed: "And I look for the resurrection of the dead and the life of the world to come" right along with the church.

But the difference is that the church lived within the joy of knowing that this promised future resurrection of the dead *had already begun*. The dawn of the future age had already sent its cheering rays over the world with the resurrection of Jesus from the dead. This is what changed everything: real human flesh and blood alive forevermore on the other side of suffering and death. This makes resurrection not a mere idea about what awaits at the end of time but the solid hope that a man who was flesh of our flesh and bone of our bone, who truly died and truly was buried, was yet raised and raised in incorruption. His table companions saw Him on the other side of death, unmistakably Him, with the body marked with the wounds in hands, feet, and side. They were invited to touch and see and thus toss away all fear and doubt forevermore. You realize, then, what this meant to them: they had met the Firstborn from the dead (Colossians 1:18). No wonder He called Himself "the resurrection" (John 11:25). He is its start but not its finish, for "because I live, you also will live" (John 14:19).

What changes with the resurrection of Jesus? Everything. Absolutely everything. His risen flesh proclaims that death itself is not permanent but temporary. Now you know that you can view it just as Jesus Himself did (see Mark 5:39; John 11:11). It is but a little sleep. And easier than a mom can wake a sleeping teen, the voice of Jesus will rouse the dead, and they will live: "Do not marvel at this, for an hour is coming when all who are in the tombs will hear His voice and come out" (John 5:28–29). This coming release from death He has won for our entire race—not just for those who believe, but even for unbelievers! Everyone is going to be raised in their bodies, but as the prophet Daniel foretold: "Some to everlasting life, and some to shame and everlasting contempt" (Daniel 12:2). But either way, the resurrection of Christ truly broke the hold of death on all human nature.

The resurrection of Christ also then changes how you live. Think of the difference in the apostles once they knew that death itself was in the rearview mirror. Pre-resurrection, Peter cowered before the servant girl's inquiries (John 18:17); post-resurrection, Peter preached fearlessly to the crowds and called out the Jewish leaders for the murder of their Messiah (Acts 2:14–41; 4:5–12). Giddy in his fearlessness. Rejoicing, even, when he is beaten. This is the same man? Oh, yes! This is what happens when the joy of the resurrection takes hold. Think of how these men dedicated the rest of their days to spreading this joy from one end of the earth to the other. They wanted everyone to know that death (awful as it is) is a defeated enemy because of what Jesus had done for them by suffering on His cross to atone for their sins, dying to destroy their death, and then rising again to give them a share in His own unending, incorruptible life. So they were tortured, some of them quite gruesomely, but their resurrection joy could not be quenched, no matter what. They went to their deaths as true martyrs, witnesses to the Love that was stronger than death!

The resurrection of Jesus also changes how you think about your own body. Suddenly you realize that you are dealing with a gift from God that will be restored to you at the Last Day. What you do with and in your body truly matters. It's not something that you will ever discard for good. No, *sin* you will discard for good. But not your body.

I still remember the funerals of my wife's grandparents. It was the same pastor (not a Lutheran) at both funerals. After we had confessed the Apostles' Creed, he made the absolutely horrific statement that we leave their bodies here because "they don't need them anymore." Nothing could be further from the truth! Jesus' own resurrection reveals this. Our bodies are not discardable bits of us, like a snake wriggling out of its old skin. Heaven forbid! Our bodies are our homes in this world, and He promises that they will be our homes as well in the world of incorruption, when all things have been made new.

The resurrection of Jesus changes how you think about your sin too. St. Paul rejoiced: "That is why his [Abraham's] faith was 'counted to him as righteousness.' But the words 'it was counted to him' were not written for his sake alone, but for ours also. It will be counted to us who believe in Him who raised from the dead Jesus our Lord, who was delivered up for our trespasses and raised for our justification" (Romans 4:22–25). The one whom the Father raised in glory from the dead is the very one who had died under the load of our sin. When the Father raises Him up, this is the sure sign that our sins have been atoned for and forgiven.

Think of the high priest in the Old Testament. He went behind the veil with the blood of atonement. How did the people know that the atonement had been accepted, that forgiveness had been bestowed, save by the high priest showing himself alive to them again and bringing them the blessing of God? So Jesus, alive from the dead, is proof positive that our sins have been answered for, that His atoning sacrifice on our behalf has been accepted and avails for all eternity. The resurrection of Jesus means not only death is in the rearview mirror but also the judgment upon your sin. This is why the Risen One sent His own out with the promise: "If you forgive the sins of any, they are forgiven them" (John 20:23). The absolution is but the verdict of the last great day already spoken over your life for you to live from. This also is a gift of Christ's holy resurrection.

Can these bones live? Because of the resurrection of Jesus from the dead, you know that not only can they live, but they will live. Herbert Mueller knew that too. In that conviction he delivered his now famous and powerful essay to the 2019 convention of The Lutheran Church—Missouri Synod in Tampa, Florida.[1] We knew he would not be with us for the next convention. He knew it too. But his joy was still unquenchable because the resurrection of Jesus had changed everything for him, as well as for you and me. In that sure and certain hope of the resurrection of his body to life everlasting, he lived his life with joy. He bore his sufferings with grace and patience. He was planted in "God's acre" (as the old Germans loved to term our cemeteries) with a certain hope. His body will sleep for a while, but the day will surely come when he will live out the words of the hymn, as will you and I, should Jesus not return first:

> And then from death awaken me,
> That these mine eyes with joy may see,
> O Son of God, Thy glorious face,
> My Savior and my fount of grace.
> Lord Jesus Christ, my prayer attend, my prayer attend,
> And I will praise Thee without end. (*LSB* 708:3)

Can these bones live? With Herb and all the faithful, we shout out: "Yes! For the resurrection of Christ changes everything!"

Endnotes

1 See below, "Joy:fully Lutheran: Rejoice, Pray, Give Thanks," 147–57.

THE RESURRECTION AND CHRISTIAN PROCLAMATION

William E. Mueller

"ALLELUIA! Christ is risen! He is risen indeed. Alleluia!" All Christians cherish these words. It is the response we share in worship on Easter Sunday, at funerals, and on other occasions. It gives us entrance into understanding and living the truth of Jesus' bodily resurrection from the dead. Because Jesus physically rose from the dead, *every* aspect of our life—our past, our present, and our future—is radically changed. This includes our preaching.

Thirty-one years ago, I was a first-year seminary student taking his first class in homiletics, the class that begins to teach the science and art of preaching. My classmates and I learned this seminary definition of homiletics: "Authoritative public discourse based on a biblical text, *centered in the death and resurrection* of Jesus Christ, for the benefit of the hearer, to the goal of faith or life." This definition is very similar to an earlier one given by Richard Caemmerer: "Preaching tells the story of Jesus Christ, namely, that He died for our sins as the Scriptures had foretold *and that He rose from the dead* according to the same predicted plan."[1] Notice the centrality of the resurrection in both definitions.

These definitions are based upon the apostolic witness given by the apostle Paul:

> Now I would remind you, brothers, of the *gospel I preached to you*, which you received, in which you stand, and by which you are being saved, if you hold fast to the word I *preached* to you—unless you believed in vain. For I delivered to you as of first importance what I also received: that Christ died for our sins in accordance with the Scriptures, that He

> was buried, that He was raised on the third day in accordance with the Scriptures, and that He appeared to Cephas, then to the twelve. Then He appeared to more than five hundred brothers at one time, most of whom are still alive, though some have fallen asleep. Then He appeared to James, then to all the apostles. Last of all, as to one untimely born, He appeared also to me. For I am the least of the apostles, unworthy to be called an apostle, because I persecuted the church of God. But by the grace of God I am what I am, and His grace toward me was not in vain. On the contrary, I worked harder than any of them, though it was not I, but the grace of God that is with me. Whether then it was I or they, so *we preach and so you believed.* (1 Corinthians 15:1–11, emphasis added)

From this Word of God notice the close connection between preaching and the resurrection. It is not just the death of Christ that preachers proclaim; the message of salvation in Jesus Christ is only complete with *the resurrection of Christ.* Paul goes on to say that "if Christ has not been raised, then our preaching is in vain and your faith is in vain" (1 Corinthians 15:14). If every aspect of the Christian life is impacted by the resurrection of Jesus Christ, then most certainly Christian proclamation is centered around, informed by, and empowered by this one and same resurrection.

It would be sufficient to give a hearty "Amen" to this and move on to the next topic. However, there is more biblical material that can be mined for the purpose of extolling and magnifying the bodily resurrection of Jesus Christ. That is fancy "preacher-speak" to say there is a lot more we can learn about the connection between the bodily resurrection of Jesus Christ and regular Christian preaching. To be precise, allow me to build upon two examples of how focusing on the resurrection of Jesus Christ in good, solid, Christian preaching gives greater clarity and comfort for the Christian.

Preaching the Resurrection Keeps the Focus upon Christ

To preach the resurrection—and for the person in the pew to expect to hear about the resurrection of Jesus Christ in a sermon—keeps the focus on Christ in our Christian faith and living. To "preach the resurrection" is to preach the whole person and work of Jesus Christ. There can be no resurrection unless there is first a crucifixion. However, take away the resurrection and Jesus Christ becomes just another person executed by the ancient Romans in a most gruesome manner. Therefore, when we talk about "preaching the resurrection," we include the whole person and work of Jesus Christ *as He is clearly defined by His own resurrection from the dead.*[2]

Begin with the earliest followers of Jesus Christ, the eyewitnesses to Jesus' resurrection, and consider how they preached. It all began on Pentecost Sunday. The apostle Peter, made bold by the Spirit of the risen Christ, preached the death *and* resurrection of Jesus Christ:

> God raised Him [Jesus] up, loosing the pangs of death, because it was not possible for Him to be held by it. . . . Brothers, I may say to you with confidence about the patriarch David that he both died and was buried, and his tomb is with us to this day. Being therefore a prophet, and knowing that God had sworn with an oath to him that he would set one of his descendants on his throne, he foresaw and spoke about the resurrection of the Christ, that He was not abandoned to Hades, nor did His flesh see corruption. This Jesus God raised up, and of that we all are witnesses. (Acts 2:24, 29–32)

Soon after this, Peter and John were going up to the temple in Jerusalem to worship. A lame man was positioned to ask for whatever monetary gifts a passerby could offer. Peter boldly told him that he did not have silver and gold to give but in the name of Jesus Christ, *the Risen One*, to rise up and walk. The miracle became a focal point for an impromptu sermon from Peter. Recounting the key points in the movement of Jesus' trial and crucifixion, Peter said, "But you denied the Holy and Righteous One, and asked for a murderer to be granted to you, and you killed the Author of life, *whom God raised from the dead*. To this we are witnesses" (Acts 3:14–15, emphasis added).

A few years passed and a new missionary appeared. Paul, the former persecutor of the church, became one of the most powerful voices of the resurrected Christ. On his first missionary journey, he and Barnabas were in Antioch in Pisidia. In his message on the Sabbath day, Paul declared:

> Of this man's [King David's] offspring God has brought to Israel a Savior, Jesus, as He promised. . . . And when they had carried out all that was written of Him, they took Him down from the tree and laid Him in a tomb. *But God raised Him from the dead*, and for many days He appeared to those who had come up with Him from Galilee to Jerusalem, who are now His witnesses to the people. And we bring you the good news that what God promised to the fathers, this He has fulfilled to us their children *by raising Jesus*, as also it is written in the second Psalm, "You are My Son, today I have begotten You." And as for the fact that *He raised Him from the dead*, no more to return to corruption, He has spoken in this way, "I will give you the holy and sure blessings of David." (Acts 13:23, 29–34, emphasis added)

Paul was connecting the dots for his hearers. The resurrection of Jesus Christ from the dead is the lynchpin that holds everything together. The bodily resurrection of Jesus Christ from the dead is the center of all Christian preaching. Take the resurrection of Christ away and all preaching falls apart.

When my seminary classmates and I were taught about the craft of preaching (the aforementioned homiletics class), we were taught that sermons should have either a "Faith Goal" or a "Life Goal." A Faith Goal sermon is one in which the preacher encourages, through the biblical witness, the hearer to grow in their faith and trust in Jesus Christ. A Life Goal sermon is one in which the hearer is encouraged to grow in living the Christian faith and life in Jesus.

Take away the resurrection of Jesus Christ and *both* kinds of sermons fall apart—and fall apart *miserably*, I might add. This might seem obvious for the Faith Goal sermon. For how can one be encouraged to grow in faith in someone who is not raised from the dead? The resurrection of Jesus is absolutely critical for this type of sermon because if Christ is not raised, then we are still in our sin (1 Corinthians 15:17). If Christ is still dead, there is no redemption, no forgiveness, no hope for the future.

Take away the resurrection of Jesus and the Life Goal sermon also falls apart. How so? Let me tell you a brief story. I first discovered this story when reading a "sermon help" article for the text of Colossians 3:1–11.[3] The illustration takes us back to the movie *El Cid*, which tells the story of a Spanish knight who almost saved the kingdom of Spain from Muslim invaders. In truth, the knight died, but his men fashioned his dead body to hold his sword and appear to be alive, ready for battle. In the Hollywood version the spoof worked, and the invaders were scared away. However, in real history, the spoof fooled no one. Why? *Because the body of a dead man is a poor leader.*

Life Goal sermons rightly encourage us to live the Christian life, to do acts of kindness, mercy, love, charity, etc. Scripture is full of these references and ideas (see Galatians 5:22–23; Ephesians 4:32; Matthew 5:14–16). However, take away the bodily resurrection of Jesus Christ and all these encouragements fall flat on their face. Why? Because if Jesus is not raised from the dead, what's the point? However, because Jesus Christ is alive, truly raised from the dead, He lives in us. He is at work even now in us. He is at work calling us to faith, strengthening us through His Supper, reminding us of His claim on us in Baptism, and moving us forward into this world by His almighty, powerful Word.

Preaching the Resurrection Keeps Us Humming

The modern-day Christian apologist Lee Strobel tells an amazing story in his book *The Case for the Real Jesus*. He recounts an interview he had with someone who does not appear to have much, if any, hold to the Christian faith. At best a skeptic, at worst an agnostic (a person who neither professes faith in God nor rejects faith). A person who, according to Strobel, professes a minimal faith in God as the Creator and the "great unknown" but rejects any notion of the God of Christianity, which he describes as "a little too childlike for me."

Who is this person whom Strobel interviewed? His name will immediately stir up various reactions. His name is Hugh Hefner, founder of *Playboy*. Strobel asked Hefner about the subject of Jesus' resurrection. Hefner's reply opens a window of understanding, albeit from the mouth of an agnostic, about the implications of Jesus' resurrection. Hefner said that if "real evidence" could be brought forward concerning Jesus' resurrection, it would lead "to all kinds of wonderful things," including an afterlife.[4]

How intriguing! How close to the truth a person can be and yet so far. You can compare this "so close to the truth and yet so far" with the exclamation of the people in Lystra: "The gods have come down to us in the likeness of men" (Acts 14:11). If an avowed agnostic can figure out the implications of the resurrection, why can we be so slow?

Of course, we know the answer. It's our sin. However, the death and resurrection of Jesus Christ has had an impact upon this sin. A *huge* impact! Connecting the dots for us with our Baptism into Christ's death and resurrection, the apostle Paul writes:

> For if we have been united with Him [Jesus Christ] in a death like His, we shall certainly be united with Him in a resurrection like His. We know that our old self was crucified with Him in order that the body of sin might be brought to nothing, so that we would no longer be enslaved to sin. For one who has died has been set free from sin. Now if we have died with Christ, we believe that we will also live with Him. We know that Christ, being raised from the dead will never die again; death no longer has dominion over Him. For the death He died He died to sin, once for all, but the life He lives He lives to God. So you also must consider yourselves dead to sin and alive to God in Christ Jesus. (Romans 6:5–11)

Keeping the resurrection of Jesus Christ at the heart of all Christian proclamation keeps us Christians humming. It continues to feed and nourish us poor, miserable yet forgiven sinners. In our world there is more than enough evidence of the ways in which we can be pulled apart and away from Jesus Christ. However, when we remember—and hear in sermons—that Jesus Himself, not only the crucified but also the *risen* Christ, says, "In the world you will have tribulation. But take heart; I have overcome the world" (John

16:33), we have the ultimate source of comfort, peace, and strength to live the Christian life. Take away the resurrected Jesus and all we have is trouble and tribulation. However, the truth of the matter is far different. With the apostle Paul we joyfully exclaim: "Christ has been raised from the dead, the firstfruits of those who have fallen asleep" (1 Corinthians 15:20).

"Preaching is the means by which people hear the Gospel. It is indispensable for the church and the way in which God chooses to save some."[5] Pastor Bernhard Seter, in an unpublished essay, gives a wealth of material for connecting the implications of the resurrection of Jesus Christ with all things in the Christian's life, but especially in the area of preaching. Preaching the resurrection is far more than Easter Sunday or the Easter season or even preaching the resurrection at funerals. The resurrection is essential to every aspect of preaching. It brings the whole person of Jesus Christ to bear upon the individual sinner. Not for the purpose of terrifying them or even scaring the sin out of them, but to bring the power, authority, and loving might of God, the one true God, who has fallen in love with fallen sinners so that we might be redeemed. The resurrection of Jesus Christ is the center of all Christian preaching and gives a renewed dose of joy to the redeemed sinner.

The bodily resurrection of Jesus Christ is central to everything in life. Believing that Jesus Christ died and rose again for every man, woman, and child has a profound impact upon you. A few years ago, I came across something that, at first, startled me, but it also drove home how the resurrection of Jesus Christ changes everything, including our preaching and anticipation of listening to a sermon. Rev. Henry Gerecke is a well-remembered and well-loved pastor. At the age of fifty, he volunteered to be a US Army Chaplain in 1943, at the height of World War II. At the end of the war, because he was fluent in German, he was assigned to be one of two Army chaplains for the Nazi officials who would stand trial in Nuremberg for their crimes against humanity.[6] The book *Mission at Nuremberg* documents the efforts of the chaplain to bring the Gospel of Jesus Christ to the former Nazi officials. A few truly repented and believed; some resisted. Hermann Goering was one of those who resisted. In his last official meeting, Goering told Chaplain Gerecke that Jesus was just a smart Jew and not his Savior. Goering cheated the hangman's noose and committed suicide just hours before he was to be executed. In searching around, I came across an audio recording of Chaplain Gerecke in which he mentions something I have not found in print. Recounting his experiences at Nuremberg several years later, Chaplain Gerecke explains that when the guard noticed Goering lying on the floor of his cell and foaming at his mouth, Gerecke rushed in and boldly stated in Goering's ear: "The blood of Jesus Christ cleanseth us from all our sins" (see 1 John 1:7).[7]

No one knows whether Goering heard the chaplain's words of Gospel. There appears to be ample evidence to suggest that even if he did hear, Goering would have rejected the message and the Savior. However, that's not why I tell this story. I tell this because this is *exactly* what we should expect from someone who believes that Jesus Christ is raised bodily from the dead! Chaplain Gerecke shows that the resurrection of Jesus Christ is not just one component of many for preaching. It is at the center, the absolute core of Christian preaching, because it shines the light ever so brightly upon this eternal truth: Jesus Christ is the risen Lord and Savior of all, who has paid the price of salvation for all. The resurrection of Jesus Christ impacts and energizes all Christian proclamation and preaching. Preaching the resurrection of Jesus is not just for Easter or even for funerals. It is for every aspect of preaching.

Alleluia! Christ is risen! He is risen indeed. Alleluia!

ENDNOTES

1 Richard R. Caemmerer, *Preaching for the Church* (St. Louis: Concordia Publishing House, 1959), 5, emphasis added.

2 See the introduction to Paul's letter to the Romans, where he emphasizes Jesus' resurrection as the defining aspect of who Jesus is (Romans 1:4).

3 Kenneth R. Klaus, "Old Nature Replaced with New One," *Concordia Pulpit Resources* 8, no. 3 (1998): 39.

4 Lee Strobel, *The Case for the Real Jesus: A Journalist Investigates Current Attacks on the Identity of Christ* (Grand Rapids, Zondervan, 2007), 105.

5 Rev. Bernhard Seter in an unpublished essay titled "A Chicken Soul for the Soup." Accessed through Rev. Donald Fondow, former president of the Minnesota North District.

6 Tim Townsend's book about Gerecke is a marvelous read: *Mission at Nuremberg: An Army Chaplain and the Trial of the Nazis* (New York: HarperCollins, 2019).

7 Henry F. Gerecke, "Chaplain Henry Gerecke," posted May 10, 2014, by Rev. Scot Kerns, YouTube, 48 min., 45 sec., accessed August 28, 2024, https://youtu.be/bewLCQwkChY?si=SQIRTXU6yUgWTPmR.

THE PASTOR'S DAILY DYING AND RISING (STRUGGLE WITH SIN, DEATH, AND THE DEVIL)

Herbert C. Mueller III

PASTORS are a strange breed. I should know; I grew up in a parsonage, and I have spent the past nineteen years preaching and teaching God's Word as a pastor. Along the way, I have seen the good, the bad, and the ugly. I have learned that the pastor encounters the same struggles that every Christian encounters in his or her walk with Christ. Being a pastor is no inoculation against a daily struggle with sin, death, and the devil. As a Christian, the pastor must also daily die and rise with Christ.

Baptized into Christ, we are baptized into a war: "All newborn soldiers of the Crucified, bear on their brows the seal of Him who died" (*LSB* 837:3). It is a war like none other: "For we do not wrestle against flesh and blood, but against the rulers, against the authorities, against the cosmic powers over this present darkness, against the spiritual forces of evil in the heavenly places" (Ephesians 6:12). After He was baptized, "Jesus was led up by the Spirit into the wilderness to be tempted by the devil" (Matthew 4:1). Does the struggle depend on us? To whom can the pastor and the Christian turn for help in this struggle? Are we as alone as we feel at times?

The battles that rage in history seem to depend mightily on human effort. On May 13, 1940, Winston Churchill addressed the House of Commons for the first time as a wartime prime minister. The battle for France had exploded. Things were not going well. In just two days, Churchill would receive news from French Prime Minister Paul Reynaud that Hitler's armies had broken through the French lines and that the situation was hopeless.

Britain would have to stand alone against Nazi Germany. Amid all of this, Churchill spoke to the struggle that lay ahead, not mincing words about the cost. He committed himself and Britain to war "against a monstrous tyranny" and set forth the clear goal: "victory, however long and hard the road may be; for without victory, there is no survival."[1]

As dark and deadly as that enemy was, Christians have an enemy that desires not only our physical subjection and death but also our eternal death and subjection in hell. The tyranny that surpasses all tyranny actually happened in the garden when the world was newly made. There the ancient serpent tempted Adam and Eve to eat from the tree of the knowledge of good and evil. There our first parents decided to join Satan's rebellion. They resolved they would choose for themselves what was good and what was evil. They came to believe that the Lord God was holding back on them. They wanted to be God, to be independent, autonomous, the captains of their own souls. When the woman and then the man ate, "the eyes of both were opened, and they knew that they were naked" (Genesis 3:7). They sundered their relationship with their gracious Creator. When they heard Him coming, "the man and his wife hid themselves from the presence of the LORD God among the trees of the garden" (Genesis 3:8).

The Lord God was not slow to address the situation. He cried out to the man, "Where are you?" (Genesis 3:9). He allowed the man and the woman to speak a confession of sorts concerning what they had done. And then He gave a promise. It was a curious sort of promise. It might seem strange to our ears, but the man and the woman, and all who would believe after them, found comfort in the curse the Lord God spoke against their enemy: "I will put enmity between you and the woman, and between your offspring and her offspring; He shall bruise your head, and you shall bruise His heel" (Genesis 3:15).

Nevertheless, this event sets a pitiable pattern for us. From this fall into sin, we all lost original righteousness, the image of God our Creator. From this original sin flows all sorts of actual sins of thought, word, and deed: lust, anger, hatred, murder, adultery, theft, gossip, covetousness, rebellion. And sin demands to be paid: "The wages of sin is death" (Romans 6:23). "In the day that you eat of it you shall surely die" (Genesis 2:17). When sin is in full bloom, the fragrance of death sticks in our nostrils.

Satan always wants to destroy human life. As Jesus said, he is "a murderer from the beginning, and does not stand in the truth, because there is no truth in him. When he lies, he speaks out of his own character, for he is a liar and the father of lies" (John 8:44). If he cannot kill outright, he contents himself with the idea that he can make life pitiful with sickness and infirmity.

Pastors see this kind of thing every day. People are hurting. They have problems. They are suffering and dying. Their loved ones are suffering and dying. They come to their pastor with these hurts and problems. They desire a listening ear, a caring voice. They need to know that their Savior has not left them, but that He has promised restoration in the new heavens and the new earth.

Other times people come with their sins. They need to hear Law and Gospel. The pastor leads them to confession with the Word of God, and then pronounces the absolution, the forgiveness of sins. And still other times people come to their pastor needing reconciliation with one another. Again, they need confession and absolution, restoration and forgiveness. At other times it is the responsibility of the pastor to rebuke sin. Again, this is done for the sake of absolution, forgiveness, and restoration. All of this is necessary because of the devil's attacks.

Add to this the fact that the devil attacks the pastor too. He tempts the pastor to be too strict where he should be permissive and too permissive where he should be strict. He tempts pastors to believe that the success or failure of the church depends on the pastor. The devil oppresses the pastor with feelings of inadequacy, along with his own sin and death. The day has a finite length, and often there is not enough time, listening, energy, mental ability to go around for everyone. The apostle Paul asks the question: "Who is sufficient for these things?" (2 Corinthians 2:16).

There is a psychological condition that pastors often suffer: compassion fatigue. The daily effort to counsel, organize, manage, minister, and especially to work in stressful and traumatic situations has tremendous physical, emotional, and psychological impacts.[2] The symptoms of compassion fatigue are feelings of helplessness and powerlessness in the face of suffering; reduced feelings of empathy and sensitivity; feeling overwhelmed and exhausted by work demands; feeling detached, numb, and emotionally disconnected; and loss of interest in activities once enjoyed. I believe that most pastors have felt something like that at times.

Compassion fatigue leads to a closely related condition called burnout: "Burnout is a state of emotional, physical, and mental exhaustion caused by excessive and prolonged stress. It occurs when [someone feels] overwhelmed, emotionally drained, and unable to meet constant demands."[3] The symptoms of burnout include exhaustion, irritability, and isolation.

Unhelpful coping mechanisms emerge from compassion fatigue and burnout. Neglecting friends and family, overeating, substance abuse, alcoholism, addiction to pornography, and even darker deeds manifest. What is to be done for the pastor undergoing burnout? What is to be done for the pastor experiencing compassion fatigue? What is to be done for Christians experiencing these things?

Secular society has found various ways of dealing with compassion fatigue and burnout. Some of these strategies may be helpful. But the Christian understands that these are not just physical and psychological phenomena. Compassion fatigue and burnout are part of the consequences of sin. These are attacks from our dire enemy. He desires to steal our joy, our health, our marriages, our bodies, and our souls. And make no mistake, the devil is playing for keeps: "With might of ours could naught be done, soon were our loss effected" (*LSB* 656:2).

However, there is someone else who is playing for keeps as well: "But for us fights the valiant One, whom God Himself elected. Ask ye, Who is this? Jesus Christ it is, Of Sabaoth Lord, and there's none other God; He holds the field forever" (*LSB* 656:2). Our only hope in this battle is the one spoken of in Genesis 3:15. The promised Seed of the woman has come. He is the only one who can defeat the devil, sin, and death. The apostle John reminds us of this fact in his first letter: "The reason the Son of God appeared was to destroy the works of the devil" (1 John 3:8).

Jesus engaged in this deadly struggle throughout His earthly ministry. It seemed as if the demons were coming out of the woodwork wherever Jesus went. One such occasion is recorded for us in Luke's Gospel: "Now [Jesus] was casting out a demon that was mute. When the demon had gone out, the mute man spoke, and the people marveled" (Luke 11:14). Think about how Satan attacked the mute man. The man could not tell his wife and children that he loved them. He could not do the normal things that we take for granted every day. He could not ask to buy food at the market or speak with a friend down the street. He could not go to the synagogue and pray and sing psalms with the congregation. Exhaustion, irritability, and isolation were his daily bread.

Now what we know about demon possession and casting out demons would fill a thimble. We do know that no baptized believer in Jesus can experience demon possession. God the Holy Spirit has taken up residence in the believer. The baptized child of God has renounced the devil, along with all his works and all his ways. We do know, however, that the devil can attack and even oppress Christians: "Be sober-minded; be watchful. Your adversary the devil prowls around like a roaring lion, seeking someone to devour" (1 Peter 5:8). Our reason is no help in understanding this. We might be tempted to think that we are above such thoughts. We have medical knowledge and science, which would tell us why a person cannot speak or has compassion fatigue or burnout. We do not need to blame such things on an evil spirit. But Scripture is clear that this muteness was demonically imposed upon this man. And Scripture is clear that the devil prowls after us. We must believe it. But we also must believe that the demon was no match for Jesus. The devil is no match for Him. He cast the demon out, and the man spoke freely. And all those around Jesus marveled at this.

Later, when questions arose about what He had done, Jesus described His campaign against the devil: "When a strong man, fully armed, guards his own palace, his goods are safe; but when one stronger than he attacks him and overcomes him, he takes away his armor in which he trusted and divides his spoil" (Luke 11:21–22).

The devil is the first strong man. He thought he could make this world his palace. He did so by enslaving some with false teaching, others with demon possession, and all people with their sins and with fear of death. Satan thought all his goods were safe. He guarded them in his full panoply of armor, kitted out with the best weaponry. The devil uses our sin, our flesh, and the world to oppress us and enslave us.

But now Jesus has come. He is the Stronger Man! The devil thought his goods were safe—he thought we were kept safe from God—but Jesus came and defeated the devil, stripping him of his armor and carrying off the goods of Satan's palace. Jesus is speaking here about His entire mission, from cradle to cross to empty tomb to His ascension and second coming too. All this has completely defeated Satan.

Jesus invaded the devil's kingdom as a little child, a baby. He was born of a virgin, the promised Seed of the woman. Throughout His mission Jesus met with resistance, as we see here in Luke 11. The demons resisted Him, but He told them where to go. The people whom He came to save resisted Him, but He corrected them, patiently teaching them. All the while, He was headed somewhere. "When the days drew near for Him to be taken up, He set His face to go to Jerusalem" (Luke 9:51). The plan and purpose of God even from before the beginning of time was that the enemy would be defeated, sin wiped out, and death undone, all by the sacrifice of the Son of God on the cross. For this reason, the Second Person of the Holy Trinity took on flesh, humbled Himself, and became obedient unto death. If Satan were to accuse Him, all his accusations would be nothing. If death were to devour Him, death itself would die. If the sins of the world were placed on Him, then they would cease to demand payment, and the fragrance of life would come from the death of the Son of God.

Satan took the bait and entered Judas Iscariot, and Judas betrayed Jesus in the Garden of Gethsemane. It was all so that Jesus would win the victory over Satan and take away all the armor in which Satan trusted. Jesus took all sins upon Himself while He had a dreadful battle with Satan at the cross. There Jesus crushed all of Satan's power by removing all that Satan trusted in. He became the maximum sinner, not because He did the wrong but because He carried the sins of the world on His back. All the armor in which the devil trusted, all his flaming darts, all his malice, all his rage was spent on Jesus. The justice of God, the same justice that Satan perverted and twisted to try to damn us forever, was poured out on Jesus. Cursed is everyone who is hung on a tree (see Deuteronomy 21:22). There, naked, with a twisted crown of thorns, with nail-pierced hands and with a spear-pierced side, Jesus conquered. It was a strange and dreadful strife. But Jesus conquered. Jesus' only policy in dealing with the devil is victory.

Death swallowed Him up, but death could not hold Him. That victory was proclaimed for all to hear on that first Easter when the tomb was empty and when Jesus appeared to His disciples. He gave them the forgiveness of sins that first Easter, locking the connection between that forgiveness, that worldwide absolution, and His death and resurrection: "If you forgive the sins of any, they are forgiven them" (John 20:23). Thanks be to God! When the Lord Jesus, the Lamb of God who takes away the sin of the world, cried out, "It is finished," from His cross (John 19:30), sin's debt for all was fully paid. Satan was routed. Death was undone. Now Jesus announces this forgiveness to His disciples with that absolution.

This absolution is a trusty weapon against sin, death, and all the power of the devil. With Christ holding this trusty weapon of the forgiveness of sins at our side, we cannot fail to find comfort and peace. All of Satan's power is doomed to fail: "This world's prince may still scowl fierce as he will, he can harm us none. He's judged; the deed is done; one little word can fell him" (*LSB* 656:3). Martin Luther was apparently flexible about what the "little word" that fells Satan is. He spoke of two words. One is "Jesus": "When [the devil] hears a Christian speaking the one word 'Jesus of Nazareth' with true faith, he falls down as if struck by a thunderclap. For he burned his own fingers on Jesus, so that he can do no more harm to Him" (AE 69:264). And whatever the devil may be able to do to one who bears Jesus' name will all come to nothing too.

The other "little word" that Luther referenced is simply this: "Devil, you lie!" (AE 41:186). Therefore, the Christian can say, "Devil, you lie when you say that I am not redeemed. Devil, you lie when you say that God's wrath is not appeased by the blood of Christ. Devil, you lie when you say there is something that I must do to earn salvation. Devil, you lie when you tempt me and trick me into sin. You lie when you tell me that now that I have sinned there is no hope. Devil, you are a liar and a murderer. You go to hell, devil, for my Savior, Jesus, has conquered you. I am His and He is mine by faith."

Martin Luther expounds on this same comfort of Jesus' ultimate victory over sin, death, and all the power of the devil in his 1535 Galatians commentary. In Galatians 2:19, Paul writes: "For through the law I died to the law, so that I might live to God." Luther calls this "most delicious language" (AE 26:155). It is so delicious because the Law's accusations, the fiery darts that the devil hurls at our conscience, are all overcome and abrogated by the "law" of grace.

When attacked by sin, death, and the devil, our Ally is there to help us:

> Against my sin, which accuses and devours me, I find there another sin. But this other sin, namely, that which is in the flesh of Christ, takes away the sin of the world. It is omnipotent, and it damns and devours my sin. (AE 26:159)
>
> And so when I feel the terrors of death, I say: "Death, you have nothing on me. For I have another death, one that kills you, my death. And the death that kills is stronger than the death that is killed." . . . The more the devil attacks [the believer] with all his force and tries to overwhelm him with all the terrors of the world, the more hope he acquires in the very midst of all these terrors and says: "Mr. Devil, do not rage so. Just take it easy! For there is One who is called Christ. In Him I believe. He has abrogated the Law, damned sin, abolished death, and destroyed hell. And He is your devil, you devil, because He has captured and conquered you, so that you cannot harm me any longer or anyone else who believes in Him." (AE 26:162)

The pastor's daily dying and rising is a daily return to the cross where the sin that devours and damns sin is at work. He daily dies with the death that kills death. He daily burns the fingers of the devil with the name of Jesus, the devil that torments the devil. For this is Jesus: the sin that damns sin, the death that kills death, the devil for the devil. Whenever the pastor hears the Gospel, receives the absolution, partakes of the body and blood of Jesus, remembers his Baptism, this is what is really going on. The Son of God destroys the works of the devil. The Stronger Man is binding up the strong man and carrying away his spoils. The pastor, and any Christian, is the spoils that Jesus carries away from His victory.

There are many ways for the pastor to receive this sin-damning, death-killing, devil-defeating Word. Daily it is poured out on him through his Baptism into Christ. Often it is placed on his lips and in his mouth in the body and blood of Christ. This is also how every pastor, every Christian, should view private confession and absolution and the mutual conversation and consolation of the brothers. Pastors remind one another that Jesus conquers. Jesus waged war with all His might against our dire foe. With the body and blood of God He silences the lies of the evil one. His only policy is victory, victory for us all through His shed blood. His blood, toil, tears, and sweat, not ours. His ordeal of the most grievous kind, not ours. Amid the battle, we sing: "And when the fight is fierce, the warfare long, steals on the ear the distant triumph song, and hearts are brave again, and arms are strong. Alleluia! Alleluia!" (*LSB* 677:5). The distant song comes near; we hear the joyful lay in Word and Sacrament!

The pastor realizes that this assurance is not just for him but for all. He takes this treasure in his crushed, broken clay jar to everyone and anyone who will hear it. In joyful cheer he announces the devil's defeat, even in the face of sin and death, knowing that it is for the Stronger Man to carry away the spoils.

Endnotes

1 Winston Churchill, "Blood, Toil, Tears and Sweat: House of Commons, 13 May 1940," in *The Speeches of Winston Churchill*, ed. David Cannadine (London: Penguin, 1989), 149.

2 WebMD, "Compassion Fatigue: Symptoms to Look For," WebMD, updated December 12, 2022, accessed August 28, 2024, https://www.webmd.com/mental-health/signs-compassion-fatigue.

3 Melinda Smith, "Burnout Prevention and Treatment," HelpGuide, accessed August 28, 2024, https://www.helpguide.org/articles/stress/burnout-prevention-and-recovery.htm.

"I KILL AND I MAKE ALIVE"

Mark W. Love

See now that I, even I, am He, and there is no god beside Me; I kill and I make alive; I wound and I heal; and there is none that can deliver out of My hand. (Deuteronomy 32:39)

DO you know which God is the only God? At the time Moses sang his inspired song recorded in Deuteronomy 32, the people of God likely knew that He alone was God. The entire song reveals that the generations coming after them would forget. Although unimaginable at the time Moses was singing his song, God knew that His children's children would eventually not know Him and ultimately reject Him as the one true God. Their forgetfulness or willful ignorance would harden their hearts and bring them to practice idolatry, bowing and bending their worship, their sacrifices, and their living to something other than the true God. Although God had revealed Himself as their God and their Lord (YHWH—the saving/rescuing God) through His Word and His works, they would turn aside from the Lord (Jeremiah 5:23) when they exchanged the truth about both themselves and God for a lie (Romans 1:25). Yet God the Lord thinks on mercy, not wrath, not desiring their death, but that they would turn and live (Ezekiel 33:11). He is faithful and patient, desiring that all should reach repentance unto salvation (2 Peter 3:9). To bring them, and us yet today, to this salvation, God declares that He will "kill and . . . make alive . . . wound and . . . heal" (Deuteronomy 32:39).

To hear God declare that He will kill and make alive, wound and heal sounds like anything other than what God, a loving God, would say. Yet we must remember with whom God is dealing. Despite the illusions we may have about ourselves, because we have been conceived in sin and born in iniquity (Psalm 51:5), everyone has a stubborn and hostile sinful nature toward God. Even after we have been redeemed by God, our sinful nature constantly rebels against the Word of God, often taking us captive to sin

(Romans 7). It is in this context of the saints who have been led away from the true God by their sinful nature that God makes this declaration: "See now that I, even I, am He" (Deuteronomy 32:39).

The Hebrew for this verse is better expressed as "See now that I, even I AM, He." This "I AM" is the saving name that God used to reveal Himself to Moses and His people in Egypt. It is the name He chose to identify Himself as the deliverer of His people who were helplessly enslaved in Egypt. For He is the Lord; He is the God who, even in wrath, remembers mercy (Habakkuk 3:2). By this name, God assures His people that when they would again refuse to believe that He alone was the Lord their God and would enslave themselves in sin, He would again be to them the only God who rescues His people. He would reveal Himself as the only true God who would rescue His people by means of killing and making alive, wounding and healing. Thus the purpose of His killing is to rescue, to make alive, to resurrect, and the purpose of His wounding is to heal. This raises the question: Whom must God kill to make alive or resurrect, and whom must He wound in order to heal?

One might think that it is the unfaithful people of God who need the killing and the wounding. After all, they had the one true God, His promises, and the covenant He established with them, and yet Moses testified that they would give Him up for alternative gods, which were no gods. If anyone deserved to be killed and wounded, it was them: "What the true proverb says has happened to them: 'The dog returns to its own vomit, and the sow, after washing herself, returns to wallow in the mire' " (2 Peter 2:22). Yet having given themselves up to other gods, they had already killed themselves spiritually.

The only hope of being made alive again, of being resurrected, is by way of killing and wounding their faith in these other gods. To this end, God kills and wounds the very things that His people have made their gods. He put to death the ability of these things to be of any good, let alone a better good for them than their real God, who is the Lord. It is through killing their false gods or idols that His people's faith in them as gods would die. Only when their faith in such gods is put to death would His people be the most free to see and believe that the power of these dead gods is gone, that there is none remaining to help. It is here that God, who is faithful even though we may be unfaithful (2 Timothy 2:13), would by the Holy Spirit through His Word of promise proclaim anew that He will vindicate and have compassion on His people (Deuteronomy 32:36). He would make them alive again, resurrecting them through repentance and faith for the forgiveness of their sins to the renewal of eternal life.

One of the best illustrations of this killing and making alive is the prophet Jonah, who chose to flee from the presence of the Lord (Jonah 1–4). Jonah turned away from the Lord, choosing to believe in his ability both to reject the will of God for him and to escape the Lord's presence by fleeing to Tarshish. The purchase of his passage was a confession of faith in his cleverness and his ability to live apart from the Lord's will for him.

To kill Jonah's faith in his ability, the Lord set about killing the power of those things in which Jonah put his faith to deliver him from the will of God and His presence. The wounding and killing began with the Lord hurling the great wind upon the sea so that the ship Jonah bought passage on was threatened to the point of breaking up. Through this tempest, the Lord wounded and killed the mariners' faith in their ability to deal with it. Each began to cry out to his god in the hopes that those gods would save them and perhaps the ship, but their gods were killed by the power of this tempest. Jonah's faith was so sure in the ability of these helpless and hopeless mariners that he was down in the inner part of the ship, fast asleep.

Then the Lord began wounding Jonah's faith in his own cleverness, using the captain's rebuking question, "What do you mean, you sleeper? Arise, call out to your god! Perhaps the god will give a thought to us, that we may not perish" (Jonah 1:6). In all of this, Jonah was unwilling to enter the presence of the Lord from which he had fled, so he did not pray. While he knew why the tempest had come, he trusted in the power of his silence to save him. Yet the casting of lots killed the power of Jonah's silence to save him from his sins of disobedience and his flight from the Lord.

When asked what they were to do with him, Jonah acknowledged that the tempest threatening all their lives was the presence of the Lord seeking His disobedient and unfaithful servant. Jonah told the mariners that their only hope of being made alive again, resurrected from the storm, was for them to toss him overboard. Their only path to life again was to kill him. Unwilling to believe this, the mariners trusted in their ability to save themselves and Jonah from the presence of the Lord, so they rowed harder. The Lord then killed any faith in their ability to save themselves and Jonah by causing the sea to become more and more tempestuous. With their faith in themselves killed, they called not to their gods but to the Lord whom Jonah had revealed to them. They called out in humble submission to God and hurled Jonah into the sea. By this act of killing him, they were delivered from the raging sea.

Jonah had yet to humble himself. Neck deep in the sea, Jonah remained spiritually dead by his refusal to repent and call on the Lord. Whether Jonah believed in his ability to tread water until he made it to land or that a ship might pass by, he did not humble himself and call on the name of the Lord.

Here, the Lord stepped in to kill Jonah's faith in anything other than the Lord so that He might make Jonah alive again. Whatever illusion in which Jonah had put his faith, whatever gave him confidence enough to refuse to humble himself, the Lord put all this to death by the great fish sent to swallow him. Notice that He did not physically kill Jonah. Now, deep in the belly of the fish, God killed Jonah's ability to believe in anything other than the God who is his Lord. Only when all things and all avenues in which he might have put his faith were dead did Jonah finally humble himself before the presence of the Lord. Only with the death of all his false gods did Jonah come face-to-face with his own death. Now, in the belly of the fish, Jonah surely believed that the Lord was killing him for his unfaithfulness and sinful rebellion. Everything Jonah saw and experienced by the Lord's killing and wounding he saw as the Lord's judgment against him. Yet the Lord was using His killing and wounding to effect His work of rescue and resurrection for Jonah, a rescue and resurrection that was accomplished when the Lord had the fish spew him, body and soul, onto the beach. There the Lord renewed this dead and newly-made-alive prophet in his commission to go to Nineveh. Jonah was renewed in seeing that God is He, even "I AM," the Lord, and there is none who can take His children out of His hand.

The Lord's use of killing to make us alive follows on mankind's sinful choice of killing God to make ourselves alive by faith in other gods. The Lord's use of wounding to heal us and make whole our godless ways follows on mankind's choice to wound the ways of God. Adam and Eve wounded their knowledge of God and His ways by ignoring God's command and eating the fruit of the tree of the knowledge of good and evil. Having killed God as their Creator by their sinful faith in their ability to re-create themselves as God, they killed themselves with God.

Yet God, who is love (1 John 4:8), sets out to do what is necessary for the welfare of those He loves. God revealed to Adam and Eve, and to all their sinful children to this day, that He is unwilling to let any sinful wound or killing take those He loves out of His hand. Through His promise to use the Seed of the woman to crush the head of the serpent, even as the serpent would bruise His heel, God affirmed that He would use the killing and wounding of this Seed to save mankind. This Seed is His own Son,

Jesus Christ, whom He sent to be born of a woman, born under the Law (Galatians 4:4), to be wounded so that by His wounds we are healed (Isaiah 53:5). While we were enemies of God, His own Son was born to reconcile us to God by His death, by His killing on the cross (Romans 5:10), and through the resurrection of Christ Jesus from the dead we are born again to a living hope (1 Peter 1:3).

Through Holy Baptism, God the Holy Spirit has baptized us into the death and burial of Christ so that, just as Jesus Christ was raised from the dead, we, too, might walk in newness of life (Romans 6:3–4) through faith in Jesus Christ. This walk in newness of life is walked with our old sinful life, which is hostile to the saving blessings of God in Jesus Christ. It is in this context that God had Moses tell the people that they would return to the way of sin and unbelief. Later in Romans, Paul confesses that even though he is in the newness of his life of faith in Christ, he is again and again taken captive by the sin still with him. But God wounds and kills his sinful ways, those things other than God in which he places his confidence, and Paul confesses: "Wretched man that I am!" He knows himself as dead to God. And he asks, "Who will deliver me from this body of death?" (Romans 7:24). Here Paul is as Jonah was in the belly of the fish. Yet God who is faithful still calls him by His Holy Spirit, and like Jonah, Paul is spewed from death to life. Alive again in Christ through forgiveness, Paul shouts: "Thanks be to God through Jesus Christ our Lord!" (Romans 7:25), rejoicing that for those who are in Christ Jesus, those who humbly repent and believe in Him, there is no condemnation, no killing of them by God (Romans 8:1). It is in this that we know that God is the Lord and that no sin, no wound can take us out of His hand.

Peter explains God's purpose of killing and wounding in our lives. In the context of rejoicing because God has caused us to be born again to a living hope, Peter says, "Now for a little while, if necessary, you have been grieved by various trials, so that the tested genuineness of your faith—more precious than gold that perishes though it is tested by fire—may be found to result in praise and glory and honor at the revelation of Jesus Christ" (1 Peter 1:6–7). Peter likens our faith to gold, and God uses various trials—the killing and wounding—to prove and purify our faith. So that what remains is pure and saving faith, everything that is not of faith in Christ must be purged, must be put to death. Peter's words "if necessary" reveal that God's killing and wounding are not random or reckless but purposeful for our preservation in the faith in the only God, who is our Lord.

This God who is the Lord has caused us to be born again in Christ through the washing of rebirth and renewal by the Holy Spirit so that we might become heirs of eternal life (Titus 3:5–6). Until then, God is at work in all things, even killing and wounding, because we are called according to His purpose, that we may be conformed to the image of Christ (Romans 8:28–29). In all this, the Holy Spirit, who intercedes for us (Romans 8:27), keeps us in this faith as we await the coming of our Lord Jesus Christ, who will resurrect all flesh from the dead and "transform our lowly body to be like His glorious body" (Philippians 3:21).

JOY:FULLY LUTHERAN[1]

Rejoice, Pray, Give Thanks

Rev. Dr. Herbert C. Mueller Jr.

BELOVED Brothers and Sisters in Christ!

"Pastor," she said, "we don't want *Lutheran* theology! We want *biblical* theology." I was brought up short. I had been showing my Bible class the Lutheran approach to the book of Revelation. So I told them the reason I am Lutheran is simply that Lutheran theology *is* biblical theology.[2] We are "Joy:fully Lutheran" because our teaching from the Bible brings the greatest possible comfort for hurting and broken people. I was new in that parish, so we spent the next year or more in class exploring how every aspect of Lutheran biblical theology is *laser-focused* on bringing maximum comfort to dying sinners, that is, hurting and broken people, one and all. "With joy," as Isaiah said, we were "draw[ing] water from the wells of salvation" (Isaiah 12:3).

Clear Lutheran theology points unerringly to Christ. In the introduction to the Convention Bible Study, Pastor Tim Pauls writes, " 'Joyfully Lutheran' makes . . . sense . . . because joy is found *where Christ* is found, and Lutheran theology is all about being found *in* Christ, *with* Christ."[3]

Christ for you is the reason St. Paul could write our convention theme verse: "*Rejoice* always, *pray* without ceasing, *give thanks* in all circumstances; for this is the will of God in Christ Jesus for you" (1 Thessalonians 5:16–18, emphasis added). Christ crucified for your sins and raised again for your justification (Romans 4:25) is the *core* of our theology, the center around which everything turns:

- *Christ for you* brings joy.

- *Christ for you* enables us to pray.
- *Christ for you* is the reason we give thanks in all circumstances.
- *Christ for us* is why we *are* "Joy:fully Lutheran."

So explore with me . . . *Christ for you and for all*:

1. Christ for you at the font
2. *Christ for sinners* brings joy in forgiveness
3. [Christ for you brings] joy in vocation and witness
4. [Christ for you brings] joy in prayer, even in suffering
5. Christ for you at the altar
6. [Christ for you brings] joy even through our tears

Christ for You at the Font

Joy begins with *Christ for you* at the font. Baptism, in the Scriptures, is God's work, God's doing. The God of the universe puts His name on you, claims you for His own, unites you with His Son in His death and resurrection. There is nothing in all the universe more sure and certain than the name of the Father and of the Son and of the Holy Spirit, into whom we are baptized. God insists on having *you*! Years ago, I conducted a graveside service for a little girl—Melanie was her name—who lived thirty minutes after birth. But she was baptized! God Himself had placed His own triune name on her. With her parents, through our tears, we could revel in *Christ for us*, Christ for their little girl. So also you, all who are baptized, be comforted! Know that the triune God will never abandon His name. We may run from Him, but He always remains true to His promise. God Himself has buried us with Christ "in baptism, in which [we] were also raised with Him through faith in the powerful working of God, who raised Him from the dead" (Colossians 2:12). Is there any better comfort for dying sinners? In a soaring sermon on Baptism, C. F. W. Walther preaches:

> Should the Christian stand all day long at the grave of all the joys which he enjoyed in past years, through Holy Baptism a great stream of joy [*Freudenstrom*] has been conducted in his heart, which does not drain away, but streams forward with his life until its waves carry him into the sea of a blessed eternity.[4]

Even if everything else seems uncertain, your Baptism remains. It happened, and God does not go back on His Word.[5] This is why we bring even infants for Baptism. We want them to have the same promise of God.

The Bible is utterly clear about original sin. We sin because we are sinners through and through, and that sin leads to death. "Behold, I was brought forth in iniquity, and in sin did my mother conceive me," said David (Psalm 51:5). Thus "the intention of man's heart is evil from his youth," says God through Moses (Genesis 8:21). So Jesus taught: "Out of the heart . . . proceed evil thoughts, adulteries, murders" (Mark 7:21 NKJV). Paul writes by the Spirit: "No one does good, not even one" (Romans 3:12). In other words, the Bible teaches that sin is not simply a minor blemish on the human character. Nor is sin something we can overcome if we just try harder, with better education. No, "the wages of sin is death," says the Scripture (Romans 6:23). If sin is only a small problem, maybe all we need is a coach to give us a few helpful tips to overcome it. But I hate to tell you, none of you—not one—can wake up one morning and ultimately decide you are never going to die. We don't need a few tips. We need a Savior. If our sin problem is small, we only need a small Savior. But in *Christ for you*, we have a great Savior. We have the very Savior we need, the one who has taken all our sin into Himself, who paid for every last one, who absorbed the wrath of God we deserved, who died our death and has risen from the dead to justify us forever.

Christ for you means simply Christ for *all sinners*—real comfort for hurting and broken people.

Christ for Sinners Brings Joy in Forgiveness

All of this hangs on the fact that Jesus Christ is both fully God and fully human, God become one of us. There is a shuttle driver at the St. Louis Airport Hilton where I often park my car when flying. He sees me coming and right away wants to question me about the doctrine of the Trinity and the deity of Christ. This man is a committed Jehovah's Witness, basically a full-on Arian. That means he sees Jesus as someone special, divine in some sense, but *not* fully divine, on the same level as the Father. Jesus to him is a created being, *not* "of one substance with the Father," *not* "God of God," as we confess in the Nicene Creed. I come back with clear Scriptures such as in Christ "the whole fullness of deity dwells bodily" (Colossians 2:9). Why is this so important? As a man Jesus knows our weakness and like us lived under God's Law. Human through and through, Jesus suffers under the wrath of God for our sin and dies our death. Yet the Scriptures are abundantly clear: Jesus is at the same time the eternal Son of God, fully divine, living without sin, keeping the Law perfectly in our place. His shed blood stills the wrath of God we deserved. As God in our flesh, Jesus overcomes death and the devil and extends the fruit of His sacrifice for all. If Jesus died a mere man, there is no benefit for us. He is just another one of thousands crucified by the Romans. But because Jesus is completely human *and* at the same time "God of God, Light of Light, very God of very God, begotten, not made, being of one substance with the Father" (Nicene Creed), not only does He know what we suffer, sin could never find a foothold in Jesus, not the devil, not even death itself could ever hold onto Him.[6] He is risen from the dead, alive forevermore. Now baptized into His name and trusting Jesus, the God-man, now seated at the right hand of the Father, brings us eternal comfort, as the Bible explains:

> Since therefore the children share in flesh and blood, He Himself likewise partook of the same things, that through death He might destroy the one who has the power of death, that is, the devil, and deliver all those who through fear of death were subject to lifelong slavery. For surely it is not angels that He helps, but He helps the offspring of Abraham. Therefore He had to be made like His brothers in every respect, so that He might become a merciful and faithful high priest in the service of God, to make propitiation for the sins of the people. (Hebrews 2:14–17)

Our God intimately knows our condition and has done everything to make us His own forever. *Christ for us* is pure *joy*! In Him we find the help we need. He is God Himself in our flesh. God Himself come to pay the ransom price. So being wheeled down the hallway toward surgery, only one thing would come to my mind: the catechism I learned as a child (*say it with me*):

> I believe that Jesus Christ, true God, begotten of the Father from eternity, and also true man, born of the Virgin Mary, is my Lord, who has redeemed me, a lost and condemned person, purchased and won me from all sins, from death, and from the power of the devil; not with gold or silver, but with His holy, precious blood and with His innocent suffering and death, that I may be His own and live under Him in His kingdom and serve Him in everlasting righteousness, innocence, and blessedness, just as He is risen from the dead, lives and reigns to all eternity. This is most certainly true.[7]

I love how Martin Luther in his Galatians commentary expands on the comfort of Christ's death and resurrection. He will go off on these Gospel "riffs":

> When I feel the terrors of death, I say: "Death, you have nothing on me. For I have another death, one that kills you, my death. And the death that kills [that is, the death and resurrection of Jesus] is stronger than the death that is killed." (AE 26:162)

The devil is sent off packing as well:

> The more the devil attacks [the believer] with all his force and tries to overwhelm him with all the terrors of the world, the more hope [the believer] acquires in the very midst of all these terrors and says: "Mr. Devil, do not rage so. Just take it easy! For there is One who is called Christ. In Him I believe. . . . And He is your devil, you devil, because He has captured and conquered you, so that you cannot harm me any longer." (AE 26:162)

Wonderful consolation for hurting and broken people like us! It is the joy of the forgiveness of sins and justification by faith in Christ alone.

The apostles of Christ were totally convinced that the whole Old Testament was all about Jesus and the forgiveness of sins. For example, Peter preached: "To Him all the prophets bear witness that everyone who believes in [Jesus] receives forgiveness of sins through His name" (Acts 10:43).[8] Thus the Lutheran confessors called the doctrine of justification by faith the article by which the church stands or falls. Indeed, the Apology says the highest worship of God is to look to Jesus for the forgiveness of sins (Ap IV 154).

Think of the parts of a bicycle wheel. There's the rim and tire. There are the spokes that connect the rim with the hub. But the most important part is at the center, the axle, around which it all turns. The rim could be bent and some of the spokes might be broken, but the wheel would still turn. Without a hub and axle, though, not only will the wheel not turn, you really don't even have a wheel at all, just loose spokes and a rim. In Lutheran biblical theology the forgiveness of sins in Christ and justification by faith alone are the axle of the wheel. This is what holds everything together. If you put anything else at the center, no matter what, there's no joy. Every other aspect of our theology—creation, ethics, even the sovereignty of God—*must* revolve around justification and the forgiveness of sins. With St. Paul, "we hold that one is justified by faith apart from works of the law" (Romans 3:28). God counts me righteous for the sake of Christ. *This* is *the center* around which everything turns, the source of everlasting, never-ending joy. It is by faith in Christ alone. By faith we know God as Father. All other theological approaches steal the joy.

Being a Christian is at heart not a matter of doing but of receiving gifts. By faith we receive life and salvation in the water of Baptism. By faith we are clothed in the righteousness of Christ. By faith we receive the benefits of Christ's body and blood in the Sacrament. Everything about our theology is so arranged to give us joy in the forgiveness of sins, joy in the fact that God accounts us righteous in Christ, that He declares us not guilty for the sake of

Christ. This brings maximum comfort to hurting and broken people, penitent sinners. Again, Luther writes:

> [By faith] you are so cemented to Christ that He and you are as one person, which cannot be separated but remains attached to Him forever and declares: "I am as Christ." And Christ, in turn, says: "I am as that sinner who is attached to Me, and I to Him. For by faith we are joined together into one flesh and one bone." . . . This faith couples Christ and me more intimately than a husband is coupled to his wife. (AE 26:168)

So how is all this delivered to us? How do we come to this faith? Earlier in 1 Thessalonians Paul wrote: "And we also thank God constantly for this, that when you received the word of God, which you heard from us, you accepted it not as the word of men but as what it really is, the word of God, which is at work in you believers" (1 Thessalonians 2:13). The word translated as "is at work" is ἐνεργέω—from which we get our words "energy" and "energize." The Word of God moves. God speaks. Stuff happens. Jesus says, "Your sins are forgiven" (Luke 7:48), and it's done. Sins are forgiven. Then on Easter evening Jesus gave His church the same task: " 'Peace be with you. As the Father has sent Me, even so I am sending you.' And when He had said this, He breathed on them and said to them, 'Receive the Holy Spirit. If you forgive the sins of any, they are forgiven them; if you withhold forgiveness from any, it is withheld' " (John 20:21–23).

One of my responsibilities these past nine years has been to chair the Synod's Colloquy Committees. A Reformed Presbyterian pastor who was becoming Lutheran by colloquy described the difference this way. In his former understanding, the Word of God is information you can take or leave, like a poster on the wall. It's true, but it's up to you to accept it. So, he said, Baptism was important, but nothing happens beyond our action. The Lord's Supper is commanded, but it's only a symbol. Nothing really happens unless you make it happen.

In the Lutheran understanding, as this man was coming to know it, the Word of God does what it says. The "word of God is living and active" (Hebrews 4:12). Jesus says, "This is My body, given for you," and so it is. "My blood shed for you for the forgiveness of sins," and so it is (see Matthew 26:26–28). God's Word is not simply true information, but it actually delivers what it promises. It is energizing. It works. God's Word never returns empty, but it accomplishes God's own purpose (Isaiah 55:10–11) and delivers *Christ for us*. In the Large Catechism we confess:

> The Word is so effective that whenever it is seriously contemplated, heard, and used, it is bound never to be without fruit. It always awakens new understanding, pleasure, and devoutness and produces a pure

> heart and pure thoughts. For these words are not lazy or dead, but are creative, living words. (LC I 101)[9]

This is why there is joy in repentance. To repent is simply to admit your need for God, to turn away from sin and turn toward the Father, and to know that you have nothing without Him. Often the hardest thing we ever have to do is to admit when we've been wrong, but Jesus says there is joy before the angels of God for every sinner who repents (Luke 15:10). Repentance is worked by the Holy Spirit through the Word followed by the energizing Word of forgiveness. This is why, through the years, I've always appreciated going to a pastor when I'm troubled by sin. He helps me peel back the onion layers of my feelings to get at the root pride and idolatry. Then, sent by Jesus, he becomes the voice of Jesus Himself: "Take heart; the Lord has put away your transgression. Your sins are forgiven you!" This Word of God is not lazy or dead, but creative, living, and it does what it says and delivers what it promises! Here is real comfort for the broken, because of *Christ for us.*[10] This is why there is also . . .

Joy in Vocation and Witness

Whatever the shape of your family, it is a gift of God. Christ for us gives joy in our families. A Christian home is often the first place where the Word of God is at work in our lives to reveal His grace. We learn to forgive one another for Jesus' sake and have joy in giving and receiving God's love. In families we live out our various vocations.[11] God does not need our good works, but other people do, especially our family. God calls each of us to serve Him in His world to provide for others. Fathers, mothers, husbands, wives, grandparents, sons, daughters, workers, employers, government and other authorities are all people God uses to bring His blessings. Not one of our families is perfect, but, forgiven in Christ, God gives joy as we serve others in Jesus' name. In all our vocations, but especially in our families, we are the arms, the feet, the mouth of Jesus to love and care for others.

Baptized into His name, Christ has also made us His royal priests, giving us joy in bearing witness to Him. All the baptized are called to tell the great things God does in Christ. When folks ask the reason for the hope and joy within us, we point to Christ alone, Christ for us. When we pray "Thy kingdom come," we are not only praying that God would give us His Word and faith through that Word, we are also asking God to use even us in extending His kingdom to many more (LC III 53–54). That way we join in the joy of the angels when another sinner repents and receives the forgiveness of sins through Christ. So there is also . . .

Joy in Prayer, Even in Suffering

Because Christ is for us, our Father commands us to pray, indeed, tenderly invites us to crawl up on His lap to address Him as "Abba, Father," promising to hear. If, because of your experience, you have a hard time thinking of God as Father, come see Jesus, your Brother, praying for you in the garden: "Father, if it is Your will, take this cup away from Me; nevertheless not My will, but Yours, be done" (Luke 22:42). Because Jesus drank all the way to the bottom that cup of suffering, we can be sure the will of God is *always* for our good. That very night, Jesus had promised His disciples: "Whatever you ask in My name, this I will do, that the Father may be glorified in the Son. If you ask Me anything in My name, I will do it" (John 14:13–14). Luther has this wonderful example:

> It's like a time when the richest and most mighty emperor would tell a poor beggar to ask whatever he might desire. The emperor was ready to give great royal presents. But the fool would only beg for a dish of gruel. That man would rightly be considered a rogue and a scoundrel, who treated the command of his Imperial Majesty like a joke and a game and was not worthy of coming into his presence. In the same way, it is a great shame and dishonor to God if we—to whom He offers and pledges so many inexpressible treasures—despise the treasures or do not have the confidence to receive them, but hardly dare to pray for a piece of bread. (LC III 57)

Christ for you is reason for joy even in suffering. Far from being a sign that God has abandoned us, in the nail-scarred hands of Jesus, our crosses can be God's tool to strip away anything and everything that gets in the way of our relationship with God. Suffering, you see, has a way of crushing our idols. The saddest thing is when, in our pain, instead of clinging to Jesus, we cling to all that is crumbling before our eyes and turning to dust in our grasp, when God desires nothing more than to carry us through. At the end of the book of Job, after all Job's suffering, all his questions, all the foolishness of Job's friends, God appears to Job out of the whirlwind. He does not bring a logically reasoned-out philosophical answer for Job's questions, but He shows up. He comes. That's what we have in Christ for us. God Himself shows up to suffer with us and for us, and to conquer even death by His resurrection. This leads to . . .

Christ for You at the Altar

I learned anew the meaning of this when I had the privilege of attending worship at one of our partner churches, Jesus Lutheran Church in Riga, Latvia. During the Agnus Dei, I sensed this great movement behind me.

All the older members of the parish were surging forward. Out of respect, the younger people allowed them to approach the altar first, sometimes in walkers and wheelchairs. I thought of things they must have endured during the fifty years Latvia was ruled by the Soviet Union, when pastors were hauled off to Siberia never to be seen again simply for teaching children the catechism. These older saints were pressing forward, hungry for the "medicine of immortality," Christ's body and blood. The Lord of heaven and earth, the one with all authority and power, the one who gave Himself into death for us, who allowed His body to be broken, His blood to be poured out, the one who rose again from the dead—this one was coming to meet them in His body and blood. *What joy!* Heaven itself touches our lips! It is not that we climb up somehow to the highest heaven to find Him in our hearts, but that He Himself deigns by His Word to come down, as the angel in Isaiah with the burning coal, to touch our lips with His grace: "Your guilt is taken away, and your sin atoned for" (Isaiah 6:7). It is not a matter of our doing, but simply receiving the gifts Jesus gives.

Our joy at the altar gives a quick glimpse of the eternal joy already ours in Jesus. Our congregations are part of that assembly "in which the Gospel is purely taught and the Sacraments are correctly administered" as we confess in the Augustana (AC VII 1).[12] Our theme, "Joy:fully Lutheran," has nothing to do with a sectarian triumphalism but simply reflects the joy of living in the full and free Gospel, for there is "one Lord, one faith, one baptism" (Ephesians 4:5), which is why we joyfully confess "one, holy, catholic and apostolic Church." When Jesus gathers us around His throne, He will open our eyes to see the whole assembly,

> a great multitude that no one could number, from every nation, from all tribes and peoples and languages, standing before the throne and before the Lamb, clothed in white robes, with palm branches in their hands, and crying out with a loud voice, "Salvation belongs to our God who sits on the throne, and to the Lamb!" (Revelation 7:9–10)

Amazingly, our worship there begins here and now when we receive His body and blood.

Joy through Our Tears

Even as Holy Communion is a joyful foretaste of the feast to come, so also, every time we take one of our loved ones out to the cemetery, there can be, despite our tears, joy in Christ for us. Remember Luther saying, "Death, you have nothing on me!" Although we are staring death in the face, we truly defy that open grave when we commit the body to its resting place,

> earth to earth, ashes to ashes, dust to dust, in the sure and certain hope of the resurrection to eternal life through our Lord Jesus Christ, who will change our lowly bodies so that they will be like His glorious body, by the power that enables Him to subdue all things to Himself.[13]

We spit death in the eye whenever we confess in the Apostles' Creed: "I believe . . . in the resurrection of the body and the life everlasting."

Even now, though culture may be against us, though it may seem the leadership of our world is losing its collective mind, we can look around and see the signs foretold, remembering the words of Jesus: "When these things begin to take place, straighten up and raise your heads, because your redemption is drawing near" (Luke 21:28). Just as Jesus called Lazarus from the grave, so will He call you forth and raise you to eternal life with Him. There shall be a new heaven and a new earth where righteousness dwells (2 Peter 3:13). And God Himself will be with us as our God.

> "He will wipe away every tear from [our] eyes, and death shall be no more, neither shall there be mourning, nor crying, nor pain any more, for the former things have passed away." And He who was seated on the throne said, "Behold, I am making all things new." (Revelation 21:4–5)

Conclusion

We have taken a quick dash through the heart of Lutheran theology, which *is* biblical theology![14] *Christ for us* brings maximum comfort to broken sinners. This is what by the grace of God I've sought to proclaim and be about for forty years as a Lutheran pastor. *Christ for you*! Indeed, we are "Joy:fully Lutheran" because the core of who we are, the center of our theology, is *Christ for you, Christ for all sinners.*

Endnotes

1 Adapted from the essay presented to the 67th Regular Convention of The Lutheran Church—Missouri Synod, July 21, 2019. See *Proceedings of the 2019 (67th) LCMS Convention* (St. Louis: LCMS, 2019), 91–96.

> Editor's note: Although not directly focused on the bodily resurrection of Jesus and His followers, this essay does exemplify Herbert C. Mueller Jr.'s confession of the faith once delivered to the saints. The resurrection certainly lies at the heart of and informs everything confessed in these words!

2 Being "Joy:fully Lutheran," we accept without reservation the Scriptures as the written Word of God and the Book of Concord "as a true and unadulterated statement and exposition of the Word of God" (LCMS Constitution, Article II, LCMS 2016 *Handbook*, 12).

3 *Convention Bible Study 2019* (St. Louis: LCMS, 2019), 3.

4 The quote continues: "Should the Christian be reminded all day long that the flowers of his youth fall more and more, he stands planted by God in the water of his baptism as a palm tree which becomes greener and greener and whose leaves never wither; yes, his baptism makes death for him like a short winter's nap [Winterschlafe], out of which an eternal spring—an eternal youth—follows" (translation from Jon D. Vieker, "The Doctrine of Baptism as Confessed by C. F. W. Walther's *Gesangbuch* of 1847," STM thesis, Concordia Seminary, 1990, 49–50, brackets in original; original German, C. F. W. Walther, "Am Neujahrstage," in *Licht des Lebens: Ein Jahrgang von Evangelien-Predigten*, ed. C. J. Otto Hanser [St. Louis, Concordia Publishing House, 1905], 91).

5 See also C. F. W. Walther, *Selected Sermons*, trans. Henry J. Eggold (St. Louis: Concordia Publishing House, 1981), 107.

6 The night before He died, Jesus told His disciples: "The ruler of this world is coming. He has no claim on Me" (John 14:30).

7 SC II (*LSCE*, 17).

8 See also Luke 24:44–49; Acts 5:31–32; 13:38–40; Ephesians 1:7.

9 See Isaiah 55:11; Mark 4:20; Philippians 4:8; Hebrews 4:12. See also LC II 55 (brackets in original):

> Everything, therefore, in the Christian Church is ordered toward this goal: we shall daily receive in the Church nothing but the forgiveness of sin *through the Word* and signs, to comfort and encourage our consciences as long as we live here. . . . For we are in the Christian Church, where there is nothing but [continuous, uninterrupted] forgiveness of sin. This is because God forgives us and because we forgive, bear with, and help one another.

10 The LCMS Commission on Theology and Church Relations (CTCR) recently published a great document on the gift of Confession and Absolution: *Confession and Absolution* (St. Louis: LCMS, 2018).

11 We are assuming here the biblical understanding of marriage, that it is the union of one man and one woman for life (Matthew 19:4–9). Certainly, in this fallen world there are various forms of the family in which God can still bless us. Many children, through no fault of their own, because of death or divorce, grow up in single-parent homes. In addition, by way of contrast, the world offers various counterfeit forms with cohabitation, same-sex marriage, etc., all of which are examples of the brokenness of sin.

12 This is the Lutheran (biblical) definition of the church.

13 *LSB: Pastoral Care Companion* (St. Louis: Concordia Publishing House, 2007), 134, echoing Philippians 3:20–21.

14 If you noted that this presentation echoes in some way the line of thinking in the Augsburg Confession's first few articles (e.g., the triune name, original sin, the person of Christ, justification, the means of grace, vocation, the church, the sacraments), this was not accidental!